T0206817

A Guide to the Paris of the 1920s

The Golden Moments of Paris

by **John Baxter**

Published in the United States by:
Museyon Inc.
20 E. 46th St., Ste. 1400
New York, NY 10017

Museyon is a registered trademark.
Visit us online at www.museyon.com

Right page: Kiki with an accordionist at the Cabaret des Fleurs, Brassai, 1932

ISBN 978-0-9846334-7-0

112163

Printed in China

LES ANNÉES FOLLES

"Wars will wash over us ... bombs will fall ... all
civilization will crumble ... but not yet. Let us be
happy ... give us our moment."

Greta Garbo in *Ninotchka* (1939). Screenplay by Charles
Brackett, Billy Wilder and Walter Reisch, from a story by
Melchior Lengyel.

For every city, there is an occasional golden
moment—that vintage season when it attains a peak of
achievement, and becomes, for people of all nations, the
place they most desire to visit or whose qualities they
most strive to emulate. London of the 1870s, Victoria's
imperial capital, the city of Charles Dickens and James
McNeil Whistler; Vienna two decades later, as the
Secession remade art and Sigmund Freud redefined the
nature of man; New York in 1956, when Allen Ginsberg
wrote "Howl," Elvis Presley sang "Heartbreak Hotel,"
and Don Larsen pitched the only perfect game in World
Series history to win the pennant for the Yankees.

Paris has enjoyed many such moments, but few more
strident, seminal and flamboyant as that between the
end of World War I in 1918 and the rise of European

totalitarianism in the mid-1930s: the period known as *les années folles*—the crazy years. "Paris was where the 20th century was," wrote Gertrude Stein, one of the American expatriates whose writings helped preserve a memory of that time, like a gaudy insect embedded in the amber of nostalgia.

At times, the history of Paris between the wars can seem like a scientific discovery to which the formula has been lost. As with the evolution of jazz in the United States, the chemistry that led a few gifted individuals in Paris to develop Cubism and Surrealism is hopelessly tangled. One can chart the development of such small presses as Black Sun, Contact, Three Mountains and Obelisk, but the process by which they sprang up during the 1920s in Paris—rather than in London or Berlin or New York—and why, in publishing Joyce and Miller and Hemingway changed the direction of modern literature, stubbornly resists analysis. Woody Allen's 2011 film *Midnight in Paris* was a timely reminder that certain moments in history can only truly be understood through direct experience. As those who lived through Paris in this golden age often say—you had to have been there.

—John Baxter

CHAPER 1.   SCRAP HEAP OF THE GODS:
             MONTPARNASSE AND LES MONTPARNOS............ 8

CHAPER 2.   WILD IN THE STREETS: **LES APACHES**................. 18

CHAPER 3.   THE RUSSIANS ARE COMING:
             DIAGHILEV AND THE BALLETS RUSSES.............. 26

CHAPER 4.   "WHO WAS THAT MASKED MAN?":
             FANTÔMAS, THE VAMPIRES, AND JUDEX........... 36

CHAPER 5.   A WELL-DRSSED WAR: **PARIS IN WORLD WAR I**... 44

CHAPER 6.   THE FIRST LADY OF BOHEMIA: **SYLVIA BEACH
             AND SHAKESPEARE AND COMPANY**................... 52

CHAPER 7.   PERFUME WARS: **BOTTLING THE BLUE HOUR**..... 60

CHAPER 8.   WHERE THE 20TH CENTURY WAS:
             GERTRUDE STEIN AND HER SALON.................... 68
             —DUELLING PAINTERS: MATISSE VS. PICASSO.... **76**

CHAPER 9.   THE KINDEST CUT: **THE BOB FAD AND
             THE GARÇONNE SCANDAL**................................. 78

CHAPER 10.   A KILLER NAMED DESIRE:
             THE BUSINESSLIKE M. LANDRU......................... 86

CHAPER 11.   MONKEY BUSINESS: **SERGE VORONOFF
             AND THE QUEST FOR YOUTH**............................. 94

CHAPER 12.   FARAWAY PLACES: **THE BIRTH OF TOURISM**...... 102

CHAPER 13.   FASTER, HIGHER, STRONGER, MEANER:
             THE 1924 OLYMPIC GAMES............................. 110

CHAPER 14.   "LITTLE GIRL, CAN YOU DO THE
             CHARLESTON?": **LE JAZZ HOT**............................ 118

CONTENTS

CHAPER 15.   ARTIFICIAL PARADISES: **ABSINTHE, OPIUM, AND THE CULTURE OF FORGETTING** 130

CHAPER 16.   IN THE WHITE CITY: **THE BIRTH OF ART DÉCO** ...138

CHAPTER 17.   THE MAN WHO SOLD THE EIFFEL TOWER: **THE VICTOR LUSTIG AND STAVISKY SCANDALS** .. 146

CHAPTER 18.   AS THOUGH IT KNEW: **THE UNKNOWN WOMAN OF THE SEINE** 154

CHAPTER 19.   OF THEE I SING: **AMERICAN SONGWRITERS IN PARIS** 162

CHAPTER 20.   BLACK AS THE DEVIL, HOT AS HELL, PURE AS AN ANGEL, SWEET AS LOVE: **COFFEE AND THE CAFÉ** . 170

CHAPTER 21.   LITTLE GENTLEMEN: **GAY AND LESBIAN PARIS** . 178

CHAPTER 22.   THE RAZOR AND THE EYE: **LUIS BUÑUEL, SALVADOR DALÍ, AND SURREALISM** 186

CHAPTER 23.   THE HEAVYWEIGHT CHAMPION OF MONTPARNASSE: **HEMINGWAY'S KNOCKOUT** .. 194

CHAPTER 24.   A HALF-CRAZED CAD: **THE WILD RIDE OF HARRY AND CARESSE CROSBY** 202

CHAPTER 25.   LOVE FOR SALE: **MAISONS CLOSES AND POULES DE LUXE** 210

CHAPTER 26.   WASP AND PEAR: **THE FITZGERALDS AND THE MURPHYS** 218

THE GOLDEN MOMENTS OF PARIS: **WALKING TOURS** 228
I.   SEINE LEFT BANK WALK 230
II.   LATIN QUARTER, ST. GERMAIN AND ODEON WALK .. 238
III.   MONTPARNASSE WALK 246
IV.   TROCADERO WALK 256

CHAPTER 1

SCRAP HEAP OF THE GODS: MONTPARNASSE AND LES MONTPARNOS

Few districts of any city can boast such a transformation as Montparnasse, a garbage heap that, in the course of a century, came to be hailed as the center of the civilized world.

When, in the 19th century, seminarians from the Latin Quarter climbed up from the Seine, heading for the village of stonemasons who made and sold cheap wine, they first had to clamber over an accumulation of rubble from demolished buildings and spoil from the underground stone quarries. Worse, this was also Paris's Potter's Field, where the unknown dead lay in unmarked graves. Sarcastically, the students christened it Mont Parnasse—Mount Parnassus—after the peak in Greece where the muses lived. In 1860, Baron Haussmann's

Tsuguharu Foujita, Japanese painter and engraver (left), at a cabaret with one of his outrageous models, Kiki of Montparnasse (centre)

work gangs leveled the spoil heap and built an avenue along the hilltop to mark the southernmost border of Paris. But the name stuck. The street became boulevard du Montparnasse.

Invasion created the culture of Montparnasse. Like the first hippies in San Francisco colliding with the last of the Beats, or London's Angry Young Men bumping heads with survivors of prewar Fitzrovia, new arrivals after World War I found a colony dating back 50 years, to when Haussmann demolished the Left Bank slums. In shacks they called *estaminets*, Italian masons, powdered with stone dust, shared tables with men and women dressed like gypsies—who, since gypsies were thought to come from the German region of Bohemia, were called "bohemians."

The rival cultures settled down to an uneasy peace. In a city notorious for its insularity and suspicion of foreigners, this was a community where artist could meet writer, dancer befriend painter, model encounter poet, Surrealist consort with Impressionist, Russian seduce Greek. Some compared male behavior in Montparnasse to that of diplomats socializing in the legation quarter of a foreign country, others to gentlemen passing the evening in a brothel.

Once accepted by the Montparnos, the newcomer had no need to look further for work, shelter or sex. On her first night in Paris in 1914, British painter Nina Hamnett went to the Rotonde alone. The man at the next table introduced himself as "Modigliani, painter and Jew." The beautiful and bisexual Hamnett was soon a fixture of the community, and destined to be christened "Queen of Bohemia."

Man Ray arrived from New York in July 1921. Met at the Gare Saint-Lazare by Marcel Duchamp, he was

Amadeo Modigliani (left), Pablo Picasso and André Salmon in front of the Café de La Rotonde, 1916

taken that night to Montparnasse and introduced to the core of the Surrealist group, including André Breton, Louis Aragon, Paul Éluard and Philippe Soupault. He rented a studio on nearby rue Delambre, and met Alice Prin, aka Kiki of Montparnasse, who became his lover and model. The following December, Soupault's wife organized his first show at the Librairie Six on rue Brea. In the cafés, Ray met couturier Paul Poiret, who hired him to shoot his gowns. Jean Arp, Max Ernst, André Masson, Joan Miró and Pablo Picasso asked him to photograph their work and, in many cases, make their portraits. Both Henri-Pierre Roché, author of *Jules et Jim*, and American William Seabrook commissioned him to create erotica for their private use. His address changed from rue Delambre to rue Campagne-Première, but both geographically and intellectually he never left Montparnasse.

Group portrait of American and European artists and performers in Paris: Man Ray, Mina Loy,
Tristan Tzara, Jean Cocteau, Ezra Pound, Jane Heap, Kiki de Montparnasse, c. 1920s

Boulevard du Montparnasse marked the frontier of
what expatriates designated as The Quarter. Bounded
to the east by boulevard St. Michel (aka "Boul'Mich'"),
rue de Rennes to the west and the Seine to the north,
the Quarter was not so much a suburb of Paris as its
international colony, as alien to the city at large as Soho
was to London or Greenwich Village to New York. Life
within it had little to do with France. Few residents spoke
more than a smattering of the language, fewer still
consorted with the French. Why bother? What British
journalist Sisley Huddleston wrote of Paris in 1927 went
double for Montparnasse. It offered "everything that is
obtainable. Things of the spirit and things that minister

to bodily needs, comforts and pleasures. Everything there is to be seen anywhere is in some form to be seen [here]. It is the microcosm of the universe."

As the value of the franc dropped, foreign money flooded into the Quarter. "Those who used to come to Paris once a year come once a season," wrote Janet Flanner in 1922. "Those who stayed a month have chosen their quartier and signed a lease." Astonished at how much their dollars could buy, Americans littered franc notes onto the sidewalk among the feet of the panhandlers and prostitutes who prowled it night and day, and laughed at the desperation with which they fought for them.

Estaminets remade themselves as cafés to accommodate the growing need for places not simply to drink but also to socialize. The Select, the Rotonde and the Dôme at the intersection of boulevards du Montparnasse and Raspail, and, after 1927, La Coupole, became central to expatriate life. In their warm companionability, men and women could forget their unheated unsanitary bug-infested studios and play at being the artists they most wanted to be.

Individuals and groups adopted particular cafés. At the Rotonde, the Spaniards held an afternoon *peña* or discussion group, chaired by the day's fashionable intellectual. Germans and English preferred the Café du Dôme. On a famous occasion, Henry Miller sat at one of its tables, flat broke, drinking steadily and hoping someone would come by to pay for the coffees and cognacs represented by the pile of saucers growing steadily higher at his elbow. He was rescued by Alfred Perles, who became his closest friend and a major character in his autobiographical novels. The Select stayed open all night, a magnet for drunks, whores and assorted mysteries. In February 1929, poet Hart Crane got into a drunken brawl there over the bill, and spent six days in the Santé prison before Harry Crosby bailed him out.

In a culture where few had private phones, cafés were places to meet, to gossip, to plot, to seduce, to buy and sell, but seldom to work. Ernest Hemingway retreated to Closerie des Lilas, at the far end of boulevard du Montparnasse, to write such stories as "Big Two-Hearted River" and parts of his expatriate novel *The Sun Also Rises*. Though his characters often disparage café life, he wasn't averse to relaxing in the wicker chairs that spilled out onto boulevard du Montparnasse from the Dôme and the Select. In 1923, in "Christmas on the Roof of the World," he wrote lyrically of "Paris with the snow falling. Paris with the big charcoal braziers outside the cafés, glowing red. At the café tables, men huddle, their coat collars turned up, while they finger glasses of Grog Americain and the newsboys shout the evening papers."

Montparnasse extended for a few blocks on either side of the Raspail/Montparnasse intersection. Around the corner from the Dôme, rue Delambre was lined with small hotels and studios, the homes and working places of Amadeo Modigliani, Tsuguharu Foujita, Jules Pascin, and Isadora Duncan, who gave Foujita dance lessons in return for champagne. At the Dingo Bar on Delambre, Hemingway and Fitzgerald first met. A block further south, just this side of the Cimetière du Montparnasse, on rue Edgar Quinet, were Le Sphinx, the Left Bank's most modern brothel, and lesbian club Le Monocle. Across boulevard Raspail, on rue Campagne-Premiere, the Hôtel Istria provided a convenient drinking and fornicating venue for Picabia, Pascin, Louis Aragon and Elsa Triolet.

On the downhill side of boulevard du Montparnasse, small art galleries and ateliers clustered along rue Brea and rue de Grande Chaumière. In particular,

Café du Dôme, 1928

L'Académie de la Grande Chaumière incubated numerous talents, from Balthus, Giacometti and Calder to an arresting miscellany that included Hollywood costumier Irene Sharaff, Russian "cubo-futurist" movie and theater designer Alexandra Exter, and the sensational Tamara de Lempicka, who fled from the Russian revolution of 1917 to study in Paris, and whose flamboyant and vivid Art Déco portraits were matched by a life which even seasoned Montparnos thought gaudy.

Artists colonies inevitably attract more wannabees and has-beens than the truly creative, and Montparnasse was no exception. By the mid-1930s, most successful writers and visual artists had moved on. Many of those who remained became professional bohemians, panhandling drinks and peddling spurious reminiscences to credulous tourists. The nadir would be reached immediately after the Second World War when Kiki touted for tips around La Coupole, claiming she needed money to pay her gas and light bill, but actually to buy cocaine. She died in 1953, aged only 51. Her monument in the Cimetière du Montparnasse, not far from that of Man Ray, reads "Kiki, 1901–1953, singer, actress, painter, Queen of Montparnasse." With her death, said Foujita at the funeral, the golden days of Montparnasse were buried forever.

CAFÉ HOPPING IN MONTPARNASSE

The Dôme, Rotonde, Select and Coupole all still flourish, the first two on opposite corners of boulevards du Montparnasse and Raspail, the others a stone's throw away at 99 and 102, boulevard du Montparnasse, respectively. 10, rue Delambre, now the Auberge de Venise, is the site of the former bar Le Dingo. At 171, boulevard de Montparnasse, the Closerie des Lilas is also a going concern. (all 14th.) In all cases, however, these are now more restaurants than cafés, and, particularly in the case of Closerie des Lilas, quite costly. For further addresses in Montparnasse, see Walking Tour No. 3. Housed in the former home of painter Marie Vassilieff, who decorated one of the painted columns in La Couple, the Musée du Montparnasse at 21, avenue du Maine (15th) presents exhibitions of work by and about the area and its distinguished residents. Between 1925 and 1932, Edward Titus published a magazine called *This Quarter*, showcasing work from such artists of the neighborhood as James Joyce, Ezra Pound, Salvador Dalì and Man Ray.

CHAPTER 2

WILD IN THE STREETS: LES APACHES

In his 1932 comedy *Love Me Tonight*, Maurice Chevalier dons a black roll-neck sweater, a tight tweed suit and a droopy cloth cap to sing in the character of a Paris street gangster, the type known as an *apache*.

To tourists visiting Paris during the *années folles*, the character of the *apache*, even though the great days of street gangs had been the 1890s, was integral to the Parisian experience, along with the street-corner prostitute, the artist in a paint-stained smock, and the furtive guide selling dirty postcards. American visitors were less attracted by crime, since they had enough of it at home. However tourists from more authoritarian nations, in particular Russia, paid top prices for a glimpse of Paris's underworld where the only rules were those of force.

La Danse Apache, c. 1920: The Apache was often made to look like a physical attack

Apaches battle with French police at the Place de la Bastille, August 1904, *Le Petit Journal*

Sisley Huddlestone, long-time Paris correspondent of the *London Times*, watched them being systematically duped in what came to be known as The Tour of the Grand Dukes. "The Russians were conducted to faked *apache* dens. There were the red-aproned golden-casqued girls, and the sinister-looking *apaches* with caps drawn over their eyes. A girl dressed as a *poule* in black stockings and a slit skirt let herself be scorned, rejected and flung around the stage by a *mec* in a striped jersey, a black beret, and a look of weary contempt. In the course of the dancing, a quarrel would break out. A duel with knives would be fought. The grand dukes had their money's worth of thrills; and then the girls took off their aprons and the men donned respectable hats and went quietly home to bed."

For the last decade of the 19th century and the beginning of the 20th, gangs of young *apaches* (pronounced "ar-pash") terrorized working-class Paris, particularly the districts of Montmartre and Belleville. In 1907, police exaggerated their number as 70,000, against only 8,000 policemen. Driving home this comparison, the cover of a popular magazine showed a giant *apache*, knife in hand, looming over a troop of tiny cowering lawmen. *Apaches* combined in gangs with flamboyant names, each advertising its mastery of a particular piece of turf: the Tattooed of Ivry or the Beauty Marks of St. Ouen.

Their speciality was street robbery, for which they split into small groups. While two kept watch, one throttled the victim from behind and another rifled his pockets.

It's not clear why they adopted the name of a Native American tribe. They may have learned it from such writers about the frontier as Fenimore Cooper and Mayne Reed. More probably, they saw genuine Apaches when Buffalo Bill Cody's Wild West Show played Paris every few years from 1896, since a tribal village and simulated attacks by war parties were part of the program. The 1889 World's Fair also included an exhibit showing a "typical Red Indian" hut festooned with scalps. Lurid stories in the press described Native Americans crazed by drinking the white man's "firewater."

The uniform of the Parisian *apache* featured the same tight jacket, trousers and loose cloth cap as Chevalier, but added a horizontally striped sailor's jersey, and a gold-fringed crimson sash, which could be wrapped round the hand in a knife fight or tied on the face as a mask. Tight shoes of yellow leather completed the outfit—not forgetting the most important accessory, a short wooden-handled knife. Hand-forged by Polish cutlers, regarded as the best, it was known as a *surin*, from the Romany word *tchouri*, or an *eustache*, after Eustache Dubois, the 18th century artisan who first produced them in quantity.

Apache women, known as *lamfé*, wore gaudy blouses, brightly colored aprons over their dresses, and a black velvet ribbon around their throats. They took great trouble with their hair, but wore no hats. At a time when respectable women never went outdoors bareheaded, this omission flagrantly announced their renegade status.

Apache gangs would have been more dangerous had they not wasted so much time and effort on their wardrobe and on fighting bloody turf wars. The most notorious clash took place in 1902. Joseph Pleigneur, aka "Manda," leader of the Orteaux, and François "Leca" Dominique, chief of the Popincs, both desired a teenage prostitute named Amélie Élie, known, because of her blonde hair, as Casque d'Or—Golden Helmet. To settle the question of who should have her, the two gangs fought it out with knives and pistols through the streets of Belleville.

The skirmish enraged the establishment. That gangs should fight at all was bad enough, but that they should do so over a woman seemed particularly offensive. "For half an hour," wrote journalist Arthur Dupin, "in the middle of Paris, at high noon, two rival gangs battled for a girl, a blonde with her hair piled on her head like a prize poodle. These are the customs of the Apaches of the Far West, and a disgrace to our civilization." The police made an example of Manda and Leca. Both were sentenced to terms at hard labour in the penal colony of French Guiana, Leca for eight years and Manda for life. Leca died there. Manda survived, won early release, but never returned to France.

From left: Manda, Casque d'Or and Leca

Although the French police officially retired the term
"*apache*" in 1920, the gangs, while much depleted by
World War I, lived on. One night in the 1920s, novelist
Ford Madox Ford found himself in Montparnasse,
walking beside the walls of the Santé prison, "a long
boulevard, lined all the way with high, blank, very
grim walls, darkened by the chestnut trees then newly
planted, with very dim gas-lamps far distant one from
the other.

"Fifty yards behind my back, running footsteps
sounded. I ran like hell. But they gained and gained on
me. I stood at bay under a gas-lamp, beneath the black
walls of the prison.

"They emerged from the gloom—two men. They were
apaches all right; there were the casquettes with the
visors right down over the eyes; the red woollen mufflers
floated out, the jackets were skintight, the trousers
ballooned out round the hips, and one of them had an
open jackknife."

Fortunately for Ford, they were after a rival gang
member, and didn't stop to rob or murder him.

Jacques Becker's French film *Casque d'or,* 1952

Amélie Élie lived blamelessly until 1933, and died of tuberculosis. Any slurs on her character were eclipsed by her growing legend. Obeying the principle that history repeats itself, first as tragedy, then as farce, the mystique of the *apache* survived as a dance. In 1910, dancer Maurice Modvet visited the Caveau des Innocents, a dive near the old Les Halles markets. During the evening, a *mec,* or pimp, grabbed one of the *poules,* or chicks, and performed a variation on the "Rough Dance," a country romp in which a couple playfully bumped and jostled one another. The pimp and whore made it more like a brawl, the girl begging for attention, he shoving her away, even throwing her to the floor, only to have her crawl back and clutch his leg adoringly. Impressed, Modvet paid the man to teach him the steps, and created the Apache Dance, which became a feature of nightclub shows around the world.

FROM THE STREETS TO THE STAGE

Casque d'Or inspired novels, plays and, in 1952, a film starring Simone Signoret. Over the years, sentiment softened the edges of a sordid story. In the film, Leca is a greedy middle-aged owner of a *guinguette*, or outdoor dance hall, and Manda a peaceable ex-gang member who's retired to become a carpenter. Manda kills Leca for the noblest of reasons, but is sentenced to the guillotine. Amélie, determined to be with him to the end, rents a room overlooking the prison yard in order to see him beheaded.

A 1927 guidebook reported on the status of the *apaches*, who congregated on rue de Lappe (11th). "Not tough any more. You are safe here, because, outside every resort, there stands a gendarme. Seldom, if ever, any disorder. A long dark lane of Apache Dance Halls. The noise, terrific. An uproar of mechanical pianos, banjos, drums, accordions, laughter, boisterous stamping and hand clapping. The *Apaches* are making merry. They dance, not alone with their girls but 'man with man' and always with their hats on."

CHAPTER 3

THE RUSSIANS ARE COMING: DIAGHILEV AND THE BALLETS RUSSES

For the aristocracy and intelligentsia of Russia and the Balkans at the start of the 20th century, France was a second home. In Moscow and St. Petersburg, French was the language of polite conversation. So many Russians wintered on the Côte d'Azur that the city of Nice built an Orthodox cathedral to serve them. Paris had another, just as large, and a Russian cemetery besides.

Russian ballet and theater had followed France ever since Jean-Baptiste Landé founded the Imperial Theatre School in 1738. When Serge Diaghilev launched his Ballets Russes in 1909, to base it in Paris made perfect sense. But he didn't anticipate that the Slavic passion of its composers, designers and dancers would, in the company's brief life, influence performance everywhere.

Vaslav Nijinsky with Tamara Karsavina, with whom he danced in 1911, in one of the most famous ballets of the time, *Le Spectre de la Rose*

Diaghilev (right) and John Brown, New York, 1916

The Diaghilev family got rich brewing vodka in the
provincial city of Perm but moved to fashionable
St. Petersburg, where young Serge flourished in its
cultured high society. The most powerful influence
on his life was an affectionate and artistic stepmother
on whom he doted. Even after bankruptcy ended their
lavish lifestyle—their dining table seated fifty—a small
inheritance allowed Serge to maintain a fingerhold on
that privileged existence.

He flirted with musical composition until the great Rimsky-Korsakov called his first efforts "ridiculous." After that, he immersed himself in art history. He was almost 30 before he realized that his knowledge of art and music, access to aristocracy and its money, and regiment of theatrical and artistic friends, mostly, like himself, gay, fitted him perfectly for the role of impresario.

In 1908, after mounting successful exhibitions of new European art in Russia, he persuaded his patrons to back a season of concerts, art shows and operas in Paris, all 100 percent Russian. Applauded by French critics, in the pampering of whom Diaghilev showed true entrepreneurial flair, his productions, particularly of Mussorgsky's epic historical opera *Boris Godunov*, electrified Paris's staid art establishment.

The season lost money, but one couldn't ignore its critical success. How to exploit it? Audaciously, Diaghilev selected the neglected and discredited field of ballet.

Joan Acocella, a modern historian of dance, writing in *The New Yorker*, has dismissed early 20th century ballet as "a decadent, frivolous business—a pantie parade." A few companies plodded along, replicating classic productions with antiquated choreography. Swans in tutus danced with fairies, none showing any more emotion than a wax doll. Except as props and supports for prima ballerinas, male dancers had almost disappeared.

In this moribund world, such Ballets Russes productions as the 1910 premiere of *Scheherazade* at the Paris Opera exploded like a grenade. To the sensuous music of Rimsky-Korsakov, an Arabian queen and her handmaidens enjoy an orgy with her black slaves until

Michel Fokine and Vera Fokina in *Scheherazade*, 1913-1914

Costume sketches by Leon Bakst for *Scheherazade*, 1910

all are butchered by her furious husband. Choreographer Michael Fokine wrote the libretto with Léon Bakst, who also designed the sets and costumes. Dancing the role of the queen's favorite, the Golden Slave, the athletic young Vaslav Nijinsky, Diaghilev's lover, dazzled audiences. Paris's most elegant gays clustered in the wings, competing to sponge down his sweating body as he staggered exhausted off stage.

For years, European painters had sneaked sex and violence into their work by setting their subjects in exotic oriental locales, but Diaghilev was the first to do so with theater. As Rimsky-Korsakov's music swooped and soared, the costumes and décor of Bakst and Alexander Benois swamped the stage in color. Most striking of all, the bodies of the dancers, no longer constrained by formal movements or traditional costumes, writhed erotically. The composer's widow protested that his music had never been intended to be danced to, least of all in such gaudy bad taste. She relented as *Scheherazade* became the most popular of all his works.

Bakst's vivid sets and costumes made him a star overnight. Diaghilev invited Paris's most successful painters, including Edouard Vuillard, Georges Seurat and Pierre Bonnard, to attend rehearsals. They were uniformly enthusiastic. Diaghilev hailed Bakst, then 44 and convinced he would never achieve fame, as "the hero of our ballet." Bakst wrote his wife that "Serge embraced me and kissed me in front of everyone, and the whole ballet exploded into applause and then set about chairing me on their shoulders."

Scheherazade fever swept Paris. The Musée des Arts Decoratifs bought Bakst's original sketches, dress shops advertised gowns in *etoffes Scheherasades*— Scheherezadian fabrics. Actresses asked him to create costumes, and Paul Poiret, Paris's most fashionable couturier, paid 12,000 francs for 12 designs. When someone asked Bonnard if the Ballets Russes had influenced his work, he replied, "But they influence *everyone*!"

Success brought Diaghilev little satisfaction. Living in a succession of hotel suites, increasingly ill from the diabetes he perversely refused to treat, and haunted by the dire predictions of fortune tellers, he bullied his collaborators as tirelessly as he drove himself. Photographs that show a tall, overweight man with a plump, puffy face and incongruous moustache convey nothing of his furious drive and violent temper. All agree that in the flesh he was terrifying. Dancers quailed, and even his closest collaborators avoided confrontations.

Such power made it relatively easy to impose abrupt changes on the company. Aware that, if he continued to showcase Russian passion, his productions risked becoming as predictable as those they replaced, he broke boldly with his past. Harems and oriental fantasies disappeared, along with the sensual music of Rimsky-Korsakov and Borodin. Replacing them were the jagged rhythms of the young Igor Stravinsky's *Firebird*, *Petrushka* and the notorious *Rite of Spring*, the Paris premiere of which in 1913 caused a near riot, in part because of the choreography by Nijinsky, who was already showing symptoms of schizophrenia. Massine replaced Nijinsky as Diaghilev's lover, pushing him even closer to madness.

In 1917, Diaghilev agreed to a tour of the United States. As astrologers had foretold his death on water, he stayed in his cabin for the entire voyage. In New York, he was confronted by complaints that *Scheherazade* and *L'Apres-midi d'une Faune* were "immoral." In particular, censors objected to male dancers in black body makeup embracing white women, and he was forced to make cuts. His autocratic manner angered staff at the Metropolitan Opera House. "He detested our democratic ways," grumbled one. When an exasperated Serge struck a stage manager with his cane, the man's team nearly beat him up. Later, a lead weight crashed from a stage tower, close enough to slice the impresario's bowler hat. Malice was suspected but never proved.

Diaghilev sat out World War I in Rome, luring such collaborators as Stravinsky and Prokofiev to the city as needed. Picasso and Cocteau came, bringing their outline of a short ballet to music by Erik Satie. Inspired by the circus, *Parade* would have Cubist sets and costumes. Cocteau's libretto called for the sound of a typewriter, Morse code, a dynamo, sirens, a locomotive, an airplane, and a passage played by banging on milk bottles filled to different levels with water. Recognizing the publicity value if such a facetious ballet was performed in wartime, Diaghilev told them to start work. He wasn't disappointed. The first performance caused a fuss, particularly since Fokine's choreography incorporated such dances as the one-step, until then seen only in American minstrel shows. Picasso's Cubist costumes metamorphosed into twelve-foot-high sculptures like walking billboards. *Parade* became, literally, the hottest ticket in town as couples seeking sensation rented private boxes to have sex during performances.

Moving the company to Monte Carlo, Diaghilev continued to order new work from Stravinsky and Satie while also commissioning composers of the avant garde, including George Auric and Francis Poulenc. The best young French artists—Matisse, Braque, Van Dongen, Derain, and of course Picasso—provided costumes and sets, while the choreography was often by Massine and the young Georges Balanchine. In particular *Le Train*

Le Train Bleu, stage frontcloth by Picasso for the Ballet Russes, 1924

Bleu of 1924, set on the Côte d'Azur, with a Cocteau libretto, Picasso designs and costumes by Coco Chanel, set the signature of the Ballets Russes on 1920s dance and design.

In 1928, Diaghilev visited Villa Grimaldi in Menton, where pseudoscientist Serge Voronoff claimed to rejuvenate patients by transplanting chimpanzee organs. Another guest, Francis Pastonchi, described his "large bull head that weighs down upon a squat and neglected body. But the forehead has the space for the winds of thought. The eyes seem to glaze over when he is silent, but, when he speaks—almost with an effort, squeezing the phrase between full lips—they suddenly come alive, and, oddly, always look beyond the person he addresses, as if to pursue colorful if fleeting visions."

Neglect of his health caught up with Diaghilev in 1929—significantly in Venice, a city built on water. Boils brought on by his diabetes became infected, and blood poisoning set in. He was alone in Venice with his protégé Boris Kochno, later the lover of Cole Porter. Relations with his friends and collaborators had deteriorated. He fell out with almost all his old Russian friends, including Stravinsky, and, though he often spoke of visiting post-revolutionary Russia, never saw his native country again. "Poor Serge died on bad terms with those who should have been his best friends," wrote conductor Ernest Ansermet, "and alone—in short, like a vagabond." Coco Chanel helped pay for his funeral, and for his suite at the Hôtel des Bains de Mer, since the great impresario died, as he lived, in luxury, but dead broke.

THE LAST CURTAIN CALL

Diaghilev is buried on Venice's cemetery island of San Michele, as is Stravinsky. Nijinsky died in 1950 after a long mental illness. His grave in Montmartre Cemetery is marked by a statue of him in the costume of the puppet Petrushka, commissioned by the choreographer Serge Lifar whose grave is in the Russian cemetery in Sainte-Genevieve-des-Bois. The Library/Museum of the Opera Garnier contains many documents, costume designs, scale models and other memorabilia of the Ballets Russes, including those of Bakst and Benois.

The 1948 film *The Red Shoes* by Michael Powell and Emeric Pressburger was inspired by the Ballets Russes. Leonid Massine plays the ballet master Grischa Ljubov, while Albert Bassermann, as designer, Ratov reflects Bakst's importance to the company. As Lermontov, Anton Walbrook is more personable than Diaghilev, and heterosexual besides, but otherwise gives the performance of his career as the inspired–but fatally jealous impresario–to whom ballet is "a religion."

CHAPTER 4

"WHO WAS THAT MASKED MAN?": FANTÔMAS, THE VAMPIRES, AND JUDEX

To go masked has always been a metaphor for man's ambivalent nature. Both liberating and inhibiting, the mask can hide the face of evil, mute the glory of the divine, or aid the trickster in duplicity. In particular, the domino, covering only the area around the eyes, became the favored disguise of modern malefactors. But how many know that the comic book and movie characters who wear it—Batman, The Spirit, The Shadow, the Phantom of the Opera, even the Lone Ranger—do so because of a villain born in 1911 in Paris?

FANTÔMAS: cover of the first edition of the book, which launched the celebrated masked master-criminal

His name was Fantômas.

Fantômas (pronounced 'Fanto-*marz*') first saw the
light—or, rather, the dark—in February 1911, as the star
of pulp novels by Pierre Souvestre and Marcel Allain.
The cover of the first issue became instantly iconic. A
giant masked man in white tie, tails and a silk hat looms
over night-time Paris, bloody dagger in hand. He could
be stepping over the window sill into a room where
someone sleeps—except that the sleeper is the city and
all who live there. In his steady, amused gaze one sees all
the ambivalent glamour of organized evil.

Reading the first lines of *Fantômas*, buyers were not
disappointed.
"What is Fantômas?"
"No one—and yet, yes, it is someone."
"And what does this 'someone' do?"
"Spreads terror!"

Fantômas was as good as his word. A force for mindless
violence, he inflicts evil as much for pleasure as profit.
Acid replaces perfume in the dispensers of a department
store and poisoned bouquets are sent to cabaret stars.
He sets loose giant pythons and plague-infected rats.
Floors open beneath his victims, plunging them into
hidden rivers. Others suffocate when a room fills
with sand. Trains are derailed, liners sunk, buses sent
crashing through the walls of banks, admitting masked
apaches brandishing pistols. Loyal to nobody, Fantômas
punishes a disobedient henchman by making him the
human clapper in a giant bell. As it tolls, blood splashes
to the streets, mixed with the precious stones he has
stolen.

Fantômas doesn't have it entirely his own way. He's
opposed by the dogged Inspector Juve, who never
manages to corner him, and is in fact often outfoxed. In

one novel, Juve is jailed, suspected of being the very villain he pursues. If the bumbling Juve reminds us of Inspector Clouseau in the *Pink Panther* films, Fantômas, in his effortless malevolence, resembles Professor John Moriarty, arch-villain of the Sherlock Holmes stories. Moriarty, who first appeared in 1893, may have partly inspired Souvestre and Allain, who also drew on the character of Arsene Lupin, the gentleman jewel thief and master of disguise created by Maurice Leblanc in 1905.

To readers in 1911, however, Fantômas and his thousand *apache* street thugs would have suggested only one thing—the Bonnot Gang. The *bande a Bonnot* rampaged across France in 1911 and 1912. Long before such American bandits as John Dillinger and Bonnie and Clyde, they employed automobiles in their daring daylight bank raids; the press originally called them "The Auto Gang." Yet they had no use for money. Anarchists, they hoped by attacking the financial system to destabilize society. Decisions within the group, which included five women, were made collectively: Jules Bonnot, whom the press assigned as leader, was simply a spokesman. Teetotallers and vegetarians, unemotional and remorseless, they were ready to die for The Cause. In them, Europe experienced its first taste of modern political terrorism.

In contrast to their evil creation, the inventors of Fantômas were wimps. Young lawyers turned journalists, they were co-editing an automobile magazine when the publisher Fayard put out a call for writers who could produce a novel a month in a series that would break into the lucrative working-class market.

The ordinariness of Souvestre and Allain helps explain their success. Even if they had nothing in common with Fantômas, they knew what appealed to the average reader. Writing alternate chapters, they recited their text

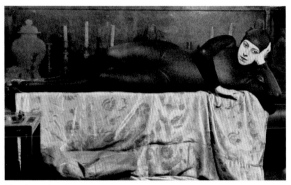

Musidora as Irma Vep in *Les Vampires,* 1915

aloud into Dictaphones for transcription by secretaries. As there was no time to read each other's work, they often had only a vague idea of the story.

As with Sherlock Holmes and James Bond, the movies made Fantômas. During 1913 and 1914, Gaumont produced a series of Fantômas serials. All were directed by Louis Feuillade, who was no more like their villain than were Souvestre and Allain. Middle-aged, conservative, a family man with a handle-bar moustache, he was brought up a strict Catholic and spent four years in the cavalry. While sharing the authors' right-wing values, however, he sensed that audiences both dreaded yet secretly craved mindless violence. As critic David Thomson observes, "He foresaw that people who went into the dark to participate in stories, no matter how sophisticated their world, were still primitive creatures."

When Souvestre, only 39, died in 1914, Allain carried on, and even invented some new characters—none, however, with the glamor of Fantômas. Instead, Feuillade created *Les Vampires*, a criminal gang that carried off its flamboyant crimes with a dash of theatricality and sex. Ballet dancers, stage performers and acrobats joined the cast. The 10 episodes of *Les Vampires* last seven and a half hours during which the forces of law and order, led by an investigative reporter, pursue the gang as its members murder, rob and kidnap.

Audiences came to know Feuillade's signature, an incongruous mixture of futuristic fantasy, crime-fighting and drawing-room melodrama. In the first episode of *Les Vampires*, an employee of the newspaper who steals the journalist's dossier on the Vampires does so because he needs money to keep a new baby, with a wet nurse, in the country. Just as the journalist forgives him, a headless body is reported found in a swamp. In a modern film, the next shot would show the reporter standing over the corpse. Instead, Feuillade has him check in with his boss and collect a chit for travel expenses. Then he drops by the house he shares with his mother, who has packed his overnight bag. As they embrace, she remembers an old family friend living near the crime scene, and insists on writing down the name and address. Later, the reporter dutifully makes a social call.

Feuillade's most ingenious invention for *Les Vampires* is a female gangster who calls herself, in a not-very-challenging anagram, Irma Vep. Daringly dressed in a skintight black body stocking, Irma flits in and out of the story, running rings round police and reporters. Played by former acrobat Jean Roques, who renamed herself Musidora, Irma and her outfit created a sensation at a time when women were expected to dress in multiple and voluminous layers of heavy clothing.

By now, Paris's intellectuals, and in particular the Surrealists, had discovered Feuillade. Rene Magritte, Robert Desnos, Guillaume Apollinaire and Blaise

Cendrars all praised the films. The suburban villas of *Les Vampires*, with secret passages, cellars where kidnapped bankers were held, and where glowing messages appeared on walls, showed, in the words of poet Paul Éluard, that "there *is* another world—but it is in this one." Revering dreams and spontaneity, the Surrealists relished the fact that Feuillade was no intellectual, and never analyzed what his biographer called "the strange, surrealist flashes of anarchy which spark through the work of this pillar of society [and] can only be explained as some sort of unconscious revolt to which he gave rein in his dreams."

France's wartime bureaucracy was less enthusiastic. The propaganda ministry accused Feuillade of further alarming a public already spooked by zeppelin raids and artillery bombardment. It briefly banned *Les Vampires*. Hurriedly, Gaumont produced a new serial, *Judex*. Its mysterious and all-powerful hero, wrapped in a black cloak and masked by a dark hat, wasn't a criminal mastermind like Fantômas, but a vigilante who used his minions and skill at disguise to punish evil-doers and redress wrongs. Shrewdly, Feuillade moved his settings out of Paris and into the countryside. Children, animals and orphans took center stage. *Judex* is *Les Vampires* as seen by the newspaper employee who stole to pay his wet nurse.

When the war ended, Feuillade launched one more shocker, *Tih-Minh*. Set in Nice, it shows the Vampires regrouping on the Riviera, swindling wealthy gamblers and dealing in drugs. Filming in casinos, depicting high-stakes gambling and semi-naked women stoned on hashish, *Tih-Minh* offered a glimpse of the sinful delights that awaited France during the crazy years into which the nation was about to descend: a world in which Irma Vep, the Vampires and Fantômas might feel completely at home.

THE CAST OF CHARACTERS LIVES ON

Feuillade died in Nice in 1925. He's buried in the cimetière Saint-Gérard in Lunel, Herault, where a high school has been named in his honor. His true monument is the films of Fantômas and the Vampires, both of whom he made immortal. Aside from numerous movies, radio and TV adaptations, the Souvestre and Allain books are still in print, while a number of new novels have used their characters. Fantômas also inspired the criminal genius Doctor Mabuse in the novels of Norbert Jacques, adapted by Fritz Lang and Thea von Harbou into a highly successful series of films.

Among more recent imitators, George Franju's film *Judex* (1963) sensitively recreated Feuillade's original, respecting the rural setting but retaining the allure of a Musidora look-alike in the person of Francine Berge, who fills a cat suit to even more erotic effect. Musidora was again rivaled by Maggie Cheung in Olivier Assayas's 1996 *Irma Vep*, playing a star of Asian action cinema who comes to Paris from Hong Kong to act in a remake of *Les Vampires*.

Louis Feuillade, 1915

CHAPTER 5

A WELL-DRESSED WAR: PARIS IN WORLD WAR I

At 11am on November 11th, 1918, an end finally came to the conflict British author H.G. Wells optimistically labelled "the war that will end war." Along 500 miles of trenches zigzagging across France from Belgium to Switzerland, the guns fell silent. Britain, France, the United States and its allies had lost 9,407,136 soldiers and civilians in the war, the Austro-German Central Powers 7,153,241—five percent of their populations. Yet the so-called Western Front had barely moved since the Germans flooded into France in August 1914.

Since the Germans got within 40 miles of the city before the British and French halted their advance, Parisians lived for four years with the war in their back garden. Artillery was often audible on the boulevards. Commanders complained of tourists wandering into the war zone, hoping for a closer look. In August 1914, American novelist Edith Wharton visited France's

Paris fashion, 1914

A girl flicking away zeppelins, *La Vie Parisienne*, April 1915,

border with Alsace, and peeked over the mountain crest at the German batteries. Troops shot at them, so they ducked back onto the French side and opened their picnic baskets.

Zeppelin bombing raids were commonplace, but Parisians shrugged them off. In April 1915, *La Vie Parisienne*, the *Playboy* of its day, showed a girl flicking away zeppelins as if they were party balloons. As always in Paris, fashion was of paramount importance. The editors gave fashion tips on what to wear in an air-raid shelter. They recommended an ermine-trimmed evening coat over your nightgown. And, you could borrow a cap from your chauffeur. Even in the trenches, soldiers tried to soften the war for their girls back home. Noting that German flares had small silk parachutes attached to slow their descent, they risked death to retrieve them. From two such parachutes, a girl who was good with a needle could sew a pair of knickers. Four gave enough silk for a blouse.

On leave in Paris, French soldiers were surprised to see few women in mourning. As no fashion-conscious Parisienne wanted to wear black for a year, the bereaved decided mourning was defeatist. "The invincible certainty of final triumph," wrote Marcel Proust, tongue in cheek, "permitted them to substitute satins and silk muslins for the earlier dark cashmere, and even to wear their pearls."

French officers, no less fashion-conscious, had their uniforms retailored in cashmere and silk, while also subtly improving the cut. For draft dodgers, the same tailors ran up quasi-military outfits smart enough to fool anyone but an expert. Once pilots appeared in the bars and clubs wearing high leather boots, riding breeches and fitted jackets, their style created a vogue. Police reported "two 'aviators' in make-up, wearing outrageously tight trousers, which roused the hostility of passersby and some *poilus*." There were more at the American cocktail bar in the Grand Hôtel on rue Auber, "dressed in fantastic uniforms, with no badges indicating their unit, and wearing their kepis tilted on the back of their heads, like jockeys."

As Paris was expensive, British troops were given only five days' leave there, not the usual 10. Also, officers had

French soldiers guarding a subway entrance in Paris, c. 1914-15

preference, since they had more money and often spoke
a little French. Most enlisted men preferred London.
All the same, many Australians, knowing this could be
their last chance to see the French capital, spent their
leave visiting those museums and historical sites that
remained open.

With bombing raids by Gotha bombers a regular event,
cinemas and theaters were given the option, providing
they displayed a notice in the foyer, of halting or
continuing performances during a raid. Most continued.
An Australian lieutenant experienced an air raid at
the Folies Bergère in 1918. "The Huns raided the city
whilst we were in the music hall and dropped a bomb
about one block away. The girls and women were very
frightened and some of the men too and it looked as if
they would start a panic but some French officers saved

the situation by asking the orchestra to continue playing and got everybody to clap their hands and cheer and do anything to keep the minds of the people away from the danger. A number of soldiers kept a large section of the crowd busy by dancing and singing."

One venue everyone expected to honor the tradition of "The show must go on" was the Grand Guignol, which staged sadistic melodramas of torture, mutilation and murder. However, the siren halted even its performances. The problem wasn't audiences but actresses. Women used to miming having their eyes gouged out with a hat pin or their face pressed to a red hot stove could imagine all too well the effect of a bomb landing in the stalls, and headed straight for the cellar at the first wail of a siren.

Paris brothels, cabarets and such variety theaters as the Folies Bergère flourished, their *promenoirs* or strolling lounges popular pick-up spots. An Australian soldier visiting the Folies Bergère in 1917 complained that "throngs of girls—some very beautiful—infest the place and persistently keep pestering you, clinging on to your belt and having to be beaten off almost."

Most French soldiers didn't have to visit the Folies to find a girl. An introduction bureau called Agence Iris offered to advertise on their behalf for *marraines de guerre*—godmothers of war. These women would promise to write to soldiers in the trenches, knit them socks, scarves and mittens, and send them small treats. They would also welcome the men if they paid a visit while on leave. In practice, the women, often widows or wives with husbands at the front, offered much more than tea and sympathy. A cartoon in *La Baionnette*, one of the humor magazines that sprang up to amuse the troops and keep up morale at home, showed an obviously gratified woman in bed chatting with a young man in uniform. "Well, you found my bed easily enough, 'nephew'," she says. "Yes," he says, "at the front I'm attached to the unit that feels out the lay of the land."

Gangsters gravitated to the rich pickings of a city at war. They included numerous *rastaquouères* or *rastas*. Suave foreigners, usually from the eastern Mediterranean or Latin America, these men dressed fashionably, had enough money to live well and the manners to move in society. Many gambled for a living. Some dealt in drugs. Others worked as gigolos or pimps. They clustered around the Opera, where, in a phrase of one chronicler, "a varied fauna had taken over the cafés and bars."

Throughout 1918, the city suffered its worst battering of the war from the Paris-Geschütz or Paris Gun. Hidden in a forest 40 miles northeast of Paris, it had a barrel as tall as a 10-story building. The 228-pound projectile left its barrel at a mile a second. Within a minute and a half, it had climbed 24 miles, to the edge of space. Three minutes after firing, the shell plunged, faster than sound, onto a theater, a school or a church.

The United States belatedly entered the war in June 1917, though it took many months for the force to reach fighting strength. Arriving with a token contingent, General John Pershing, as a symbolic act, marched to the tomb of the Marquise de Lafayette, who had fought with Washington in the War of Independence. When one of his officers announced "Lafayette, nous voilà." (Lafayette, we are here), Parisians cheered, but without enthusiasm. Three years of fruitless war had stifled their spirits.

During the winter of 1917-18, mutiny swept through the French army. Taking Pershing and his staff on a tour of the front line, Marshal Philippe Petain, the French commander, murmured "I just hope it isn't too late."

Although ruthless executions had forced rebellious troops back into the trenches, Petain feared that his men, as those of Russia had done, might simply throw down their weapons and walk away.

Though the entry of the United States tipped the scale, what finally defeated Germany was exhaustion. Food, munitions, money and men ran out. But France was no less depleted. Of the war, Edith Wharton wrote, "Like a monstrous landslide, it had fallen across the path of an orderly laborious nation, disrupting its routine, annihilating its industries, rending families apart, and burying under a heap of senseless ruin the patiently and painfully wrought machinery of civilization." The Paris that emerged was a different city. In 1914, it had set the world standard in good taste, discretion and elegance; qualities emblematized by the flowing design style known as Art Nouveau. Little of that survived the war. The Paris of 1919 was more coarse, grasping and poor; a perfect seed bed for that gaudy flowering of jazz, booze and sex known as *les années folles*—the crazy years.

SEE IT: WAR MONUMENTS

Because France capitulated during World War II, most cenotaphs and memorials refer to the War of 1914-1918. Lafayette's tomb is in the Picpus cemetery (35, rue Picpus, 12th.) The Russian cemetery at Sainte-Genevieve-des-Bois contains monuments to Russian victims of the war, including those who died at Gallipoli in the Dardanelles. A wall plaque on rue Ecole de Medecin (6th) remembers doctors who fell in combat. American pilots of the Lafayette Escadrille and other flying forces are commemorated by a memorial at Marnes-la-Coquette, about 20 minutes outside Paris.

CHAPTER 6

THE FIRST LADY OF BOHEMIA: SYLVIA BEACH AND SHAKESPEARE AND COMPANY

Few booksellers can claim to have changed the course of literature, but Sylvia Beach is one of them. This Presbyterian minister's daughter founded and ran the English-language bookshop Shakespeare and Company in Paris from 1921 to 1942. She also published James Joyce's *Ulysses*. The experience cost her dear, but her support for literature and for Paris's expatriate writers, in particular Joyce, never wavered.

Born in Baltimore on March 14, 1887, Beach was christened Nancy, but preferred Sylvia. (She also habitually amended her birth date, to 1896.) In 1901,

James Joyce and Sylvia Beach standing outside of Shakespeare and Company, 1920

her father, the Rev. Sylvester Beach, became assistant minister of Paris's American Church. The Beaches lived in Paris from 1902 to 1905, when Sylvester became pastor in Princeton, New Jersey. In 1914, Sylvia defied American neutrality, joining Ernest Hemingway, John Dos Passos, E.E. Cummings and others who volunteered to fight for France. Having no practical skills, she was sent to harvest grapes and wheat in the Loire valley, then to Belgrade, where she "distributed pajamas and bath towels to the valiant Serbs."

Back in Paris in July 1919, she gravitated to the literary world around the colleges of the Sorbonne, and in particular to rue de l'Odéon. Because of its closeness to the university, this short street near the Luxembourg gardens housed numerous teachers and students, and supported a number of bookshops. Among them was La Maison des Amis des Livres (The House of Friends of Books), owned by the bohemian daughter of a well-connected literary family, Adrienne Monnier. One day, Sylvia's wide Spanish hat blew off, and Adrienne retrieved it—the beginning of a life-long partnership.

Though Sylvia and Adrienne sensed an instant bond, it was an attraction of opposites. Sylvia was short, trim and severe, a furious smoker, with—as Hemingway noted—excellent legs. Monnier dressed in fitted velvet vests that drew attention to her pretty heart-shaped face, while voluminous ankle-length skirts disguised her overall dumpiness. From a distance, noted one writer, she resembled a farm worker standing knee-deep in ploughed soil.

When Sylvia proposed returning to New York to open a shop selling French books, Monnier, more shrewd than her new friend, urged her to remain in Paris and start an English-language bookshop instead. With $3000 from her mother, Sylvia leased a former laundry on rue

Dupuytren, around the corner from rue de l'Odéon, and stocked it with books. She called the shop Shakespeare and Company, and commissioned a hanging sign of the playwright, which also became the shop's trademark.

In May 1921 she relocated at 12, rue de l'Odéon, just across the street from Monnier. Her two-room shop had an apartment above, which was occupied at various times by avant garde composer George Antheil, and, during World War II, by Samuel Beckett and his mistress. Beckett had worked for the resistance, and hid there from the Gestapo while waiting to flee south.

In 1921, Sylvia and Adrienne moved in together, sharing a fourth floor apartment at 18, rue de l'Odéon. Shortly after, Sylvia met James Joyce at a party. "Is this the great James Joyce?" she asked nervously. Wanly, Joyce confirmed "James Joyce," and "put his limp, boneless hand in my tough little paw."

No British or American company dared publish Joyce's novel *Ulysses*. An American magazine, *The Little Review*, had been prosecuted for trying to serialize it. "What a dark age we are living in," Sylvia wrote sarcastically to a friend, "and what a privilege to behold the spectacle of ignorant men solemnly deciding whether the work of some great writer is suitable for the public to read or not!"

Quixotically, she offered to publish the book herself. Joyce agreed, but insisted on a division of income that made financial loss certain for Sylvia. So great was her respect for him, however, that she didn't argue, even when Joyce continued to travel everywhere by taxi and both dine and drink well. "The report is that he and all his family are starving," wrote Hemingway, "but you can find the whole Celtic crew of them in Michaud"—an expensive restaurant. Because of Joyce's demands,

Sylvia Beach and Adrienne Monnier at Shakespeare and Company

the first edition of *Ulysses* would sell for more than a British schoolteacher earned in a month. Most of the 1000 copies went to speculators or wealthy collectors attracted by its bawdy reputation.

Fearing English-speaking printers would refuse to set the text, Sylvia sent the book to Maurice Darantiere in Dijon, none of whose staff understood English. As a result, the first printings were riddled with typographic errors. At the same time, she printed a leaflet inviting supporters to buy copies in advance. Writer and publisher Robert McAlmon, who had typed up and edited Joyce's manuscript, touted the book among Montparnasse's café crowds, shoving any completed order forms through the shop's letterbox as he returned home. "Another hasty bunch," he wrote on one occasion. When McAlmon compiled a collection of his short stories and invited ideas for a title, Joyce proposed dryly, "How about A Hasty Bunch?" Respecting his genius, McAlmon accepted the suggestion.

Sylvia found herself working as unpaid agent and business manager for the half-blind, slow-moving Irishman, and informal gatekeeper to the other stars of Paris's expatriate literary world. She fielded mail for them, and guarded their privacy. Canadian writer Morley Callaghan, arriving in Paris in 1929, asked Beach for the address of his old colleague Ernest Hemingway. She refused to supply it, suggesting he write a letter, which she would forward.

When Scott Fitzgerald confessed he was too much in awe of Joyce to approach him, Sylvia invited both to dinner. On being introduced, Fitzgerald dropped to one knee, kissed Joyce's hand, and declared, "How does it feel to be a great genius, sir? I am so excited at seeing you, sir, that I could weep." Fitzgerald made a crude sketch of the event on the flyleaf of a first edition of *The Great Gatsby.* It shows him on his knees to Joyce, who's represented by just a moustache, spectacles and a halo. Sylvia and Adrienne are mermaids.

Ulysses was finally cleared for publication in the U.S. in 1934. Dishonestly, Joyce sold the rights to Random House, giving Beach nothing. Friends helped her apply for a government grant to support the shop. When that failed, André Gide formed the Friends of Shakespeare, members of which alone were admitted to readings. Their subscriptions helped keep the business afloat.

In 1937, Adrienne became romantically involved with young photographer Gisele Freund. Sylvia moved back into the shop apartment, and later to a bigger one in the same building. Shakespeare and Company remained open until 1942, when Sylvia angered a German officer

Sylvia Beach in her apartment, where she hid her book stock during the war, 1945

by refusing to sell her only copy of *Finnegans Wake*. After he threatened to confiscate her stock, close the shop and intern her, Sylvia's friends hurriedly painted out the name on the façade and, using laundry baskets, transferred the stock to a vacant apartment upstairs.

The Germans did later intern Sylvia for six months, but she survived the war and, though in poor health, was able to welcome Hemingway when he arrived in 1944 with his piratical platoon of cameramen and journalists to "liberate" Odéon. Before agreeing to the reunion, however, Hemingway, always nervous about his image, demanded Adrienne's assurance that Sylvia had not collaborated with the Nazis.

Except for a symbolic few days in 1944, Shakespeare and Company never reopened. The wooden façade was removed. Subsequently, the premises housed a Chinese gift store, a jeweler and a number of clothing boutiques but never another bookshop. In 1955, Monnier, increasingly tormented by an inner ear infection that caused delusions, committed suicide. The following year, Sylvia published *Shakespeare and Company*, a rambling memoir. In it, she wrote "My loves were Adrienne Monnier and James Joyce and Shakespeare and Company;" ironically, all three, in one way or another, betrayed her.

THE REMAINS OF SHAKESPEARE & CO.

The first Shakespeare and Company was at 8, rue Dupyteren. La Maison des Amis des Livres occupied 7, rue de l'Odéon (all addresses 6th). Sylvia, Adrienne, and Shakespeare and Company have no monument in Paris. A small stone tablet on the wall of 12, rue de l'Odéon commemorates the publication of *Ulysses*. If Sylvia survives, it is in the proliferation of Shakespeare and Company bookshops all over the world.

Sylvia died in 1962 and was buried in Princeton, N.J. The Princeton College Library holds her papers. She "bequeathed" the shop's name to George Whitman, American proprietor of Le Mistral bookshop, opposite Notre Dame, who bought some of her stock when she closed down. Whitman relaunched Le Mistral as Shakespeare and Company in 1964. It is now owned by his daughter, whom he named, in tribute to his mentor, Sylvia Beach. Some books from the lending library remain at the shop. Others are in the American Library in Paris.

CHAPTER 7

PERFUME WARS: BOTTLING THE BLUE HOUR

"There was a peculiar smell that emanated from the coffeehouse terraces of Montparnasse," wrote author Frederick Kohner of Paris in the early 1920s, "and I only have to close my eyes to bring it all back to me; the rich mixture of cigarette smoke, garlic, hot chocolate, *fine a l'eau*, burned almonds, hot chestnuts, and—all pervading—the strong scent of a perfume that had just become the rage of Paris—L'Heure Bleue."

Kohner is correct in all but his timing. Jacques Guerlain first marketed L'Heure Bleue—The Blue Hour—in 1912. Its arrival on the market signified a fundamental change in the use of personal fragrances.

Perfumes had existed since Egyptian times. In the Middle Ages, the French, by virtue of their mastery of gardening and an intimate understanding of the flowers that grew around such southern cities as Grasse,

Advertisement for the classic Guerlain fragrance, L'Heure Bleue, 1930s, USA.

became skilled at using steam and oil to isolate, extract and concentrate fragrances. The work was difficult and complicated. It took 440 pounds of lavender to produce 2.2 pounds of the extract used by parfumiers.

This skill flourished during the 17th century, when the Versailles of Louis XV became known as "the perfumed court," but by the late 19th century, for any woman to wear a scent other than delicate infusions of lavender or rose marked her as "fast," while strongly aromatic musk-based perfumes were used almost exclusively by courtesans and prostitutes.

This changed early in the 20th century. Parfumier Jacques Guerlain, strolling on a summer evening by the Seine (or, in some versions of the story, along a country path), was struck by, in the words of a publicist, "the spectacle [of] nature bathed in a blue light, a profoundly deep and indefinable blue. In that silent hour, man is in harmony with the world and with light, and all the exalted senses speak of the infinite."

Painters and photographers had long recognized the *heure bleue*—when daylight becomes dusk—as the moment when natural light is at its most flattering. And yet no distiller of fragrances, however masterful his technique, had ever claimed to capture anything so evanescent as atmosphere. What Guerlain saw in his moment of revelation was not so much a method of catching magic in a bottle as a way to make money.

L'Heure Bleue owed its existence to Jicky, developed by Guerlain's uncle Aimé in 1889, and regarded as the first "modern" perfume in that it used essences created in the laboratory. One of the first odors successfully synthesized was vanilla. Both Jicky and L'Heure Bleue relied on synthetic ethylvanillin to bind a mixture of natural fragrances—among them, in the case of L'Heure

Jacques Guerlain

Bleue, carnation, ylang-ylang, anise, orange blossom,
iris, licorice, aniseed, bergamot, rose, tuberose and
violet.

The marketing of L'Heure Bleue was as inventive as
its fabrication. Guerlain enclosed a few ounces of the
perfume in a molded and gilded flaçon of Baccarat
crystal with a stopper representing an inverted but
hollow heart. For women not accustomed to expensive
perfume bottles, the container was as great a pleasure
as the scent. The company used the same bottle
for Mitsouko in 1919, emphasizing its grasp of the
increasing and paramount importance of the container
in selling perfume.

In 1920, couturier Coco Chanel entered the fragrance
business, commissioning Ernest Beaux to create a
Chanel scent. Formerly parfumier to the Russian
court, Beaux used two synthetic aldehydes, one called
Rose E.B., the other a man-made jasmine, Jasophore.

Coco Chanel, 1920

Combined with iris root and other natural fragrances,
they created a distinctive perfume that he presented to
Chanel in phials numbered one to five and 20 to 24. She
chose the fifth—less from any preference than because
she believed five was her lucky number. "I present my
dress collections on the fifth of May, the fifth month of
the year," she told Beaux, "and so we will let this sample
number five keep the name it has already, it will bring
good luck."

Almost as much effort went into designing the bottle
for Chanel No. 5 as into making the perfume. Instead of
the baroque of Lalique and Baccarat, Chanel wanted a
simplicity of material and form consistent with her dress
designs; the perfume equivalent of her trademark "little

black dress." In some versions of the legend, she based the plain oblong container on the toiletry bottles in the Charvet traveling case of her lover, Arthur "Boy" Capel. In others, it was his whisky decanter that struck a chord. In a third version, she was inspired by the configuration of Place Vendôme, as seen from her suite at the Ritz Hotel.

Initially she sold No. 5 only through her French boutiques, but that soon changed. During the 1920s, the fragrance business was transformed due to the efforts of one man, François Coty. While he agreed with Guerlain and Chanel that packaging was paramount, he also believed that good design didn't preclude mass marketing. "Coty perceived perfume as something in a lovely bottle rather as merely something lovely in a bottle," wrote Janet Flanner. "He presented scent as a luxury necessary to everybody."

An aggressive Corsican with a Napoleonic complex, Coty thrust himself into the perfume market in 1904 with a fragrance called La Rose Jacqueminot. Hawking it around Paris department stores, he had little success until, supposedly by accident, he smashed a bottle in the perfume department of one of the largest, Grands Magasins du Louvre. La Rose Jacqueminot wafted through the store. Within minutes, women were converging on the source and buying every bottle.

As a selling technique, smashing a bottle was inspired, opening the door to the modern technology of samplers and scented magazine inserts. Pressing his advantage, Coty hired glassmaker Rene Lalique to design his packaging. At the same time, he expanded into low-priced soaps, powders and eaux de toilette, and exported vigorously, in particular to the United States, with a range of powders and colognes scented with the fragrance L'Origan (oregano). Once women everywhere found they could enjoy L'Origan at a modest price, its round orange boxes with their Lalique design became world-famous.

Coty channeled his millions into politics. Virulently anti-Communist and anti-Semitic, he supported the rising Fascist movement and even formed his own paramilitary organization, Solidarite Française, with the intention of overthrowing the government. It expired with his death in 1934.

By then, mass-marketing of fragrances had become commonplace. The distinctive midnight blue bottles of Bourjois' Evening in Paris were familiar worldwide. Even Chanel bowed to commercial inevitability and licensed her perfumes. In return for 70 percent of the income, the Wertheimer company launched No. 5 and other Chanel products onto the world market. Though they were phenomenally successful, it increasingly rankled with Chanel that she received only one percent of the gross income. When war broke out, she used the French government's anti-Semitic laws in an attempt to overturn the contract. Shrewdly, however, the Wertheimers had reincorporated in Switzerland and appointed a Gentile general manager. After the war, she and the Wertheimers came to an agreement that made her one of the world's richest women. Today, Chanel remains a privately held company owned by the Wertheimer family. Its annual income is $4.2 billion.

The increased popularity of fragrances for men further transformed the perfume industry during the 1930s. While some 19th-century perfumes, such as Guerlain's Jicky, were aimed at both sexes, men avoided accusations of effeminacy by patronizing more robust "toilet waters," "colognes" or "after shaves": all diluted forms of perfume. A dash of Bay Rum, made from bay leaves and other aromatics macerated in alcohol, was considered manly, as was Old Spice, launched in 1938 and mass-marketed through the Boots pharmacy chain in Britain.

No manufacturer, however, produced the dream of all parfumiers—the scent that would drive men wild. In 1937, American parfumier Elizabeth Arden suggested her fragrances made women smell like a rolling Kentucky landscape, but "outdoorsy" didn't appear to be the answer. Perfume historians Luca Turin and Tania Sanchez have proposed the most convincing theory yet. "After years of intense research, we know the definitive answer. It is bacon."

SMELL IT: PERFUME MUSEUMS AND SHOPS

Although the most comprehensive museums of perfume are in such centers of manufacture as Grasse, Paris has a number of attractive alternatives. Opened in 1914 and restored by decorator Andrée Putnam, Guerlain's flagship boutique at 68, avenue des Champs-Elysées (8th) contains numerous reminders of the perfume industry during the 1920s and 30s. The Fragonard company maintains a museum of perfume in a 19th-century *hotel particuliare* at 9, rue Scribe (9th). Exhibits include a "perfume organ" of the kind used by parfumiers to compose new scents. Coco Chanel's original boutique, opened in 1912 at 31, rue Cambon (1st), still operates. It was here that she presented all her collections, sitting on the spiral staircase, approving each model as she passed, and only descending at the close to accept the compliments of her admirers. Her private apartment on the top floor is not open to the public, but Karl Lagerfeld, who now controls the Chanel brand, has supervised the restoration of her suite at the Ritz Hotel on Place Vendôme (1st). It is available for $4300 a night.

CHAPTER 8

WHERE THE 20TH CENTURY WAS: GERTRUDE STEIN AND HER SALON

Stately in a robe of brown corduroy, attended by Alice Toklas, her watchful "wife," Gertrude Stein was the uncrowned queen of 1920s Paris. Even her appearance reflected her regal role. "She got to look like a Roman emperor," wrote Ernest Hemingway, "and that was fine if you like your women to look like Roman emperors."

Appropriate to an empress, her pronouncements had the status of holy writ—even when a quote was wrongly attributed. She did say "Paris is where the 20th century was." However the most famous phrase ascribed to her—"you are all a lost generation"—came from a French garage owner. Most people thought this applied to the expatriate writers of the 1920s. The garage owner was actually complaining about a lazy mechanic and, by

Gertrude Stein (right) and Alice Toklas in the apartment at 27, rue de Fleurus, Man Ray, 1922

The Steins in the courtyard at 27, rue de Fleurus, c. 1905. From left: Leo Stein, Allan Stein, Gertrude Stein, Theresa Ehrman, Sarah Stein, Michael Stein. Theresa Ehrman papers and photographs

extension, the whole of French youth, which, deprived of education and prospects by the war of 1914-18, could look forward only to aimless adulthood.

Even so, no memoir of Paris between the wars is complete without an evocation of Stein's Saturday night salon at 27, rue de Fleurus. Attendance signified admittance to an intellectual and artistic elite. Stein claimed her Saturdays began because Henri Matisse would ask to bring people to the apartment to see her collection of his work. Rather than refusing, she invited him at the end of her working week. Maybe that's true. It's more probable, however, that the salon replicated one Gertrude attended in Baltimore, where she and her brother Leo lived as young orphans. Two wealthy sisters,

Claribel and Etta Cone, collected modern paintings and welcomed friends on Saturdays to admire them. The Cones befriended the Steins, and helped mold their interest in art.

After Leo bought an apartment in Paris, Gertrude joined him, and together they amassed a large collection of modern paintings. She also fell in love with Alice Toklas, Leo's secretary, a relationship of which he disapproved, calling Toklas "a kind of abnormal vampire." When Leo also disagreed over their art purchases, the Steins divided their collection, and Leo left Gertrude and Toklas to occupy the apartment.

As the fame of Picasso, Matisse and Cézanne increased, an increasingly large number of people visited rue de Fleurus to view the Stein collection. In the early years of the century, guests were almost invariably painters or art lovers, and either French or Spanish. With typical dogmatism (and indifference to punctuation), Stein wrote "Painting in the 19th century was only done in France and by Frenchmen, apart from that, painting did not exist, in the 20th century it was done in France but by Spaniards." A few Americans such as Patrick Henry Bruce and Alfred Maurer might attend her soirees, but mostly it was Braque, Matisse, Juan Gris, Picasso with his mistress Fernande Olivier, one of the models for the Cubist *Les Demoiselles d'Avignon*, as well as Marie Laurencin with her lover Guillaume Apollinaire.

Visitors passed through heavy double doors from the street, walked through the main building along a long, lofty lobby, pushed through a second set of doors to enter a garden courtyard, then crossed it to Stein's two-story apartment on the other side. No guests saw the upper floors. Socializing took place entirely in the painting-hung studio just off the garden, where Stein installed herself next to a cast-iron stove that inadequately heated

Gertrude Stein at the salon, 1920

the chilly room. Though her throne-like chair was so high that her short legs dangled, guests were in no doubt that they were at court and Gertrude was queen.

Silent, often unnoticed but always watchful, Alice exercised a steely control over the proceedings. In private, feeding her partner's appetite for food and sex, bullying her with fits of jealousy, Alice wielded more power than many realized. Picasso's companion Françoise Gilot found her "sinister," Hemingway "frightening." Mabel Dodge, American patroness of the arts and voracious bisexual, blamed Alice for ending her friendship with Stein. In 1912, during lunch, Stein sent her "such a good strong look over the table that it seemed to cut across the air to me in a band of electrified steel: a smile traveling across on it—powerful—Heavens!" Alice took the look for a flirtation and left the table. Gertrude followed, then returned to explain "[Alice] doesn't want to come to lunch. She feels the heat today." They left, and Dodge never heard from Stein again.

The wider appreciation of Picasso, Cézanne and Matisse in the early 1920s also meant Stein could no longer afford their work. She compromised with canvases by Juan Gris and a miscellany of lesser lights, some better known as illustrators or theater designers—Eugene Berman, Christian Bérard, Pavel Tchelitchew. Many of these bad guesses ended up in chilly exile in the little room that Alice had occupied when she came to live at rue de Fleurus.

With Stein's own writing now widely published and discussed, she altered the emphasis of her salon to favor authors. People still came to admire the collection but stayed to talk literature and, in some cases, to solicit her opinion and advice. These new visitors, almost all expatriate and English-speaking, included Ernest Hemingway, Scott Fitzgerald, Ezra Pound, James Joyce, Sherwood Anderson, Thornton Wilder, and Paul Bowles.

For this group, the rules of the salon changed. As Stein disliked competing for attention, the sexes were segregated. Alice, described by journalist Bravig Imbs as Stein's "sieve and buckler," separated couples, steered wives and girlfriends into the kitchen, and kept them there. This left Stein to bask in undivided male attention. Although many classic French salons followed this format, Americans bridled at its sexism. Djuna Barnes was furious when Gertrude, rather than commenting on her writing, complimented her on her legs. Adrienne Monnier and Sylvia Beach protested at being dragged into the kitchen to discuss Alice's latest gadget.

The fussy influence Gertrude and Alice exercised over some guests replicated the spinsterly way the Cone sisters patronized young Gertrude and Leo. Protégés were generously fed by Alice, an excellent cook, dosed with traditional remedies, and furnished with social and career advice—some of it eccentric. Alice, surprised to hear an American girl speaking perfect French with no accent, chided her for becoming dangerously deracinated. "You must be staying with the wrong people," she said. Young Paul Bowles, whom she and Gertrude insisted on calling "Freddy," was urged to visit Tangiers, where they had just spent a holiday. He did so, and made the city his lifelong home.

Preferring to teach by example rather than precept, Gertrude read little written by her literary guests, directing them to her own work as the ideal, and urging them to learn from paintings. Ernest Hemingway was the exception. In February 1922, he and his wife Hadley visited Gertrude to present a letter of introduction from Sherwood Anderson. The penurious young couple delighted Stein. They were soon regulars at the Saturday salons. "They treated us as though we were very good, well-mannered and promising children," said Hemingway.

Gertrude became godmother to the Hemingways' son. Ernest admitted that "it was easy to get into the habit of stopping in at 27, rue de Fleurus for warmth and the great pictures and the conversation." Stein counseled him on drinking, sex and profanity, and urged him to take a more liberal view of homosexuality. She read and criticized his stories, suggesting he refine their structure and composition by studying cubist painting. Rather than the Cubists, Hemingway preferred Cézanne, and would haunt the little Musée du Luxembourg, which housed the national collection of his work.

Alice, already resentful of this attention, was incensed when Hemingway left Hadley for Pauline Pfeiffer in 1926. Ernest widened the rift by turning against Sherwood Anderson, whose novel *Black Laughter* he parodied in his 1926 *The Torrents of Spring*. When Gertrude stood up for Anderson as "a much more

Ernest Hemingway and Elizabeth Hadley Richardson , 1922

original writer" than Hemingway, the break became complete. Thereafter, he missed no opportunity to snipe at Stein, beginning with his introduction to *This Must Be the Place*, the 1937 memoirs of Jimmie Charters, barman at the Dingo and other Hemingway hangouts. "Jimmie served more and better drinks than any legendary woman ever did in her salon," he wrote. "Certainly Jimmie gave less and better advice." His posthumous memoirs, *A Moveable Feast*, published in 1964, were patronizingly dismissive of Stein.

The salon petered out when Gertrude and Alice fled into the depths of Vichy France during the war. They returned to a different Paris. After Gertrude died in 1946, it was left to Alice to welcome what she called "the GIs with their Bill of Rights and their serious novel on the way—and more serious young Fulbright scholars who are writing tomes, doctorates." Nobody could have been a more astute and faithful guardian of Stein's memory. As Gertrude had said herself, "I can be as stupid as I like because my wife is always right."

DUELLING PAINTERS: MATISSE VS. PICASSO

While Gertrude and Leo are the members of the Stein family most often mentioned as important collectors of modern art, their elder brother, Michael, and his wife Sarah were equally influential. In 1891, Michael replaced his father as manager of the Omnibus Railway and Cable Company in San Francisco. The firm prospered, and in 1904 Michael and Sarah, now sufficiently rich to have no need to work, followed Leo and Gertrude to Paris.

They bought an apartment at 58, rue Madame, only a short walk from the apartment on rue de Fleurus occupied by Leo and Gertrude. The four Steins attended the 1905 Paris Salon d'Automne, and befriended both Henri Matisse and Pablo Picasso. Leo bought Matisse's *Woman With a Hat*, which critics had derided. Among the artists who came to rue de Fleurus to see it was Picasso.

After that, the two artists competed for Stein patronage. Picasso painted his famous portrait of Gertrude, as well as a flattering one of Leo. Matisse did portraits of Sarah and Michael, and included their son Allan in two paintings, one of them *Boy with a Butterfly Net*. The number of visitors to rue Madame soon rivalled those who went to rue de Fleurus. Sarah, however, lacked Gertrude's charm. Obsessed with Matisse, who, it was said, "she worshipped almost mystically," she attacked any visitor who did not agree on his superiority over Picasso.

From 1907, as Picasso's stocks rose with Gertrude, Matisse increasingly sided with Michael and Sarah. Sarah brought Matisse's work to America and secured commissions for him. She also urged him to open a school of painting in Paris, putting up money to get it going, and becoming his student. The Steins lent their Matisses to the 1913 Armory Show in New York, which introduced the United States to the latest in European art.

In 1926, Sarah and Michael left rue Madame for a villa built for them at Garches, on the edges of the city, by avant garde architect Le Corbusier. In the 1930s, they returned to California, settling in Palo

Henri Matisse, Edward Steichen, 1909

Alto, where Matisse visited them.

On her death in 1946, Gertrude left her paintings to Sarah's son Allan, with the proviso that Alice Toklas should have their use while she lived, and be supported by income from them, even if it meant selling some of the canvases. When Allan died before he could inherit, his widow Roubina became presumptive heiress to the collection. Detested by Alice, Roubina was described by her stepson Daniel as "a devious, hypocritical, and thoroughly unprincipled being, willing to stop at nothing to achieve her ends." In 1961, when Toklas briefly left Paris for medical treatment, Roubina broke into her apartment on rue Christine and, claiming the paintings were unsafe, removed them to a bank. Alice died in 1967, never having seen them again.

CHAPTER 9

THE KINDEST CUT: THE BOB FAD AND THE GARÇONNE SCANDAL

For women in the early 1920s, particularly in France, "bobbing" their hair by cutting it short was as blatant a symbol of revolt as putting a stud through one's tongue or sporting a tattoo is today.

The appearance of a woman's head took precedence over anything happening inside it. Nobody respectable went out in public without a hat. As for hair, it was her "crowning glory." How she wore it signified social and sexual status. Young girls wore theirs either loose and flowing, or in braids. The moment when they were permitted to pin it on top of their heads signified adulthood. To "bob," therefore, expressed contempt not only for style but the entire social order.

Top: Clara Bow in *It* (1927); left: Colleen Moore in *Flaming Youth* (1923); right: Irene Castle, c.1914

Rival styles of the bob cut were hotly discussed. Parted, or with bangs? Did one dare decorate the forehead with a "spit" or "kiss curl"? Hairpins became "bobby pins" as the vocabulary of the short haircut passed into the language.

Film stars were avatars of change. Clara Bow in *It* and Colleen Moore in *Flaming Youth* flourished their bobs like banners. Exhibition dancer Irene Castle, an arbiter of fashion, endorsed the cut. "In four cases at least that I know of," she wrote, "it has been the making of a very individual and even beautiful person out of one who would not have attracted attention." Scott Fitzgerald, who'd boasted "I was the spark that lit up flaming youth. Colleen Moore was the torch," amplified Castle's comment in his 1920 story "Bernice Bobs Her Hair." Unattractive Bernice brings beaux flocking when she hints she's contemplating a haircut, and suggests some lucky boy might be permitted to watch the scissors at work. In 1920, that was more piquant than the offer of a striptease.

It took the French, however, to turn the bob into a national scandal.

The vehicle of this fuss was *La Garçonne*, a novel by Victor Margueritte published in 1922. The heroine, Monique Lerbier, is a typical daughter of a prosperous family. Pushed into an engagement, she's ready to do her duty—until she discovers her husband-to-be has a mistress. Eyes opened, she embarks on a life of excess. Stepping at random into a taxi, she offers herself to its passenger. They immediately check into one of the "hot sheet" *hotels de passe* that rent rooms by the hour.

She gets a job dancing nude in a club, flaunts elaborate costumes, including a peignoir trimmed with the plumes of the white ibis, experiments with opium, takes numerous lovers, including a female star of the music halls, and, in the ultimate act of defiance, has a child out of wedlock, whom she proposes to raise alone.

But before any of these, she first, symbolically, bobs her hair. The act announces her emergence as a new variety of individual—neither boy nor girl but a *garçonne*.

By adding "ne" to *garçon*, Margueritte feminized the word for "boy," creating a new term, poorly translated in the American title for the book, *The Tomboy*. There was nothing masculine about *les garçonnes*. Though some were bisexual, affecting short haircuts and mannish suits, most didn't dislike sex. Rather, they adopted an aggressive male attitude to it. A bob was their emblem of sexual and social liberation.

The archetypal *garçonne* was Fano Messan. Only 20 when Margueritte's novel appeared, she had been apprenticed to a number of Montparnasse artists since she was 16. Described as "the youngest sculptor in the world," she embraced the *garçonne* fashion without reserve, cutting her hair boyishly short and wearing an androgynous wardrobe. At the 1925 Salon d'Automne, she showed a piece called *Androgyne*, and was photographed standing next to it in a smock that hid everything. Lorimer Hammond reporting on the Paris art scene for the *Chicago Tribune*, wrote "The Latin Quarter amuses itself in trying to determine the sex of Fano Messan."

When Man Ray photographed Messan, he went along with the joke. In one pose, even draped in a figured shawl, wearing a mannish sweater and with her hair severely bobbed, she's obviously a girl. However, in a second pose, her body is obscured, making the question moot. When Salvador Dalí and Luis Buñuel cast her in their 1928 film *Un Chien Andalou*, they further confused

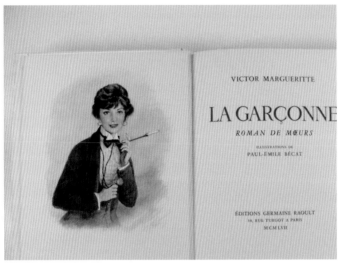

La Garçonne, Victor Margueritte, illustrations by Paul-Emile Bécat, 1957

Fano Messan, Emmanuel Sougez, 1921

things. Playing an androgynous pedestrian who pokes a severed hand with a stick, Messan is described simply as "The Hermaphrodite."

Critics continued to attack the *garçonne* style as it spread through Parisian costume and behavior. The bob cut gave birth to *cloche* i.e., bell-shaped hats (unwearable over long hair) and the "Castle Band," a bandeau over the forehead , in a style popularized by Irene Castle. Seeing a century of long hair and longer skirts swept away by rising hemlines, rolled stockings and general razzamatazz, some critics felt the devil was at the wheel.

Sociologists argued that, because of deaths during the war and the 1919 "Spanish flu" epidemic, France had 10 percent fewer eligible men. Women could no longer wait around in the hope of being selected. The doom-sayers dismissed this argument. One wrote sarcastically in 1929 "The old-fashioned ideas which so outrageously limited woman's horizon have been done away with. Now she is able to taste life to the full. She can go to night clubs. She can rub elbows with thieves, gigolos, and prostitutes. She can paint like a prostitute, dress like a prostitute, get drunk like a prostitute. At last she is free, free! Night life has changed from a man's sport to a woman's sport. It is woman who is now most active in keeping it alive. It is she who cries, 'Come on! Let's go!'"

Victor Margueritte found himself embroiled in a social and political storm. Like Vladimir Nabokov when he wrote *Lolita*, he was an improbable agent of change. In his 50s, an established editor, essayist and occasional novelist, he had been awarded, for his services to literature, France's highest civilian distinction, the *Légion d'Honneur*. Now all that was under threat.

The sexual experiment of *La Garçonne*'s heroine might have escaped censure were it not for her decision to have a child outside marriage. In deeply conservative family-oriented France, this was particularly divisive. Margueritte protested that his *garçonne* doesn't remain in revolt. At the end of the novel, she meets a man worthy of her. Not only does he believe in female equality; he throws himself in front of a jealous lover intent on murder. Independence forgotten, Monique falls into his arms. But it was too late. The Archbishop of Paris denounced *La Garçonne*. Distributor Hachette withdrew the book from railway bookstalls, a major source of sales. And finally, in a sanction usually imposed only on criminals and traitors, Victor Margueritte was formally ejected from the *Légion d'Honneur*.

In the United States, the publication of *La Garçonne* inaugurated a rash of such "bobbing" novels as Maxwell Bodenheim's *Replenishing Jessica* and *Flaming Youth* by "Warner Fabian"—actually humorist Franklin P. Adams. The moral majority responded much as it had in France. A New York grand jury tried to have H.B. Liveright prosecuted for publishing Bodenheim's novel. The attempt fizzled out, since, after the first sensation, the bob cut was accepted as just another style. As the 1920s ended, wiser heads were wondering why there had ever been such a fuss.

In her 1931 film *Shanghai Express*, Marlene Dietrich plays a sultry adventuress exercising her charms along the China coast. When, by chance, she meets a former lover, he's bitter about the time they lost. "There are a lot of things I wouldn't have done if I had those five years to live over again," he says morosely. But Marlene thinks not. "There's only one thing I wouldn't have done," she says. "I wouldn't have bobbed my hair."

THE HAIRCUT THAT CHANGED THE WORLD

The most readily recognized bob belongs to the film actress Louise Brooks. When Louise was only 10, her mother, seeing the short haircut of Gloria Swanson, cut her daughter's braids. Even in high school Louise wore her hair short, though flared out in the style known as a Page Boy or Dutch Girl. In 1928, playing a hobo in *Beggars of Life*, her disguise as a boy, in male suit, cap and short haircut, came close to the *garçonne* look. Once she achieved fame in the late 1920s, her haircut became more severe, developing into the trademark "raven helmet"—black, glossy, with straight-cut bangs across the forehead and two swerving wings across the cheeks, their points drawing attention to her expressive face with its wide eyes and questing pointed nose. A journalist of the time rhapsodized about Brooks's "camellia skin, dark eyes, and black silky hair, lucid like a Chinese varnish."

Brooks's adoption of the bob mirrored the adventurousness of her private and professional life. Feeling undervalued in Hollywood, she moved to Europe in the late 1920s, taking daring roles as a prostitute and seducer in G. W. Pabst's *Diary of a Lost Girl* and *Pandora's Box*. She never resumed a Hollywood career, and died penniless, but because of her intransigence and, arguably, her haircut—immortal.

Louise Brooks

CHAPTER 10

A KILLER NAMED DESIRE: THE BUSINESSLIKE M. LANDRU

It is only a kitchen stove, solidly constructed of black iron, somewhat rusted, obviously much used. Uncommon, admittedly, in an auction sale such as this, of objects lost and found on the railways, or surplus to government requirements, but all the same, just a stove.

So why such a crowd at this sale in Versailles on the morning of January 23, 1923? Why all these journalists? And why the presence of a tall suave man in an expensive felt hat and a coat of glossy black Persian lamb?

Bidding on the stove begins at 1000 francs. The crowd is silent. Impatiently the auctioneer raises his gavel. "Going once for one thousand … going twice …"

French serial killer, Henri Desire Landru (1869-1922), during his trial at Versailles in 1921

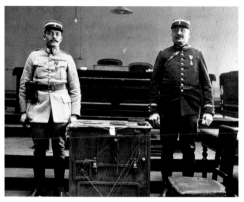
Landru's stove at the trial, 1921

"1500!" from the back of the room.
"2000!" from somewhere else.
A murmur runs through the crowd. Within seconds, the price has soared to 3700 francs.
"4200!"

It's the man in the astrakhan coat. In awed silence, the stove is knocked down to him for 4200 francs—in today's money US$6000.

As the buyer steps forward to pay, he's recognized at last. M. Anglade, director of the Musée Grevin. Well of course! Who else would pay such a fortune but the proprietor of Paris's most famous waxworks show? And perhaps it isn't so much—for the stove of Henri-Desire Landru.

Before the war, Landru had been just another swindler, earning a modest living for his wife and four children, serving short prison terms for frauds as minor as stealing bicycles and supplying inferior materials to land surveyors. Once the war arrived in 1914 and the draft swept up most able-bodied men, the opportunities of a Paris filled with lonely women proved too tempting to resist. Landru began to murder.

His unwitting accomplices were the staff of Agence Iris, a company which, for a small fee, would insert personal ads in papers and magazines, and collect replies in private boxes. Before the war, illicit lovers, prostitutes and abortionists were its main clients. Business improved once it suggested that lonely women whose men were at the front might adopt another soldier as a *marraine de guerre* or "war godmother." They could correspond with him, knit him sweaters and socks, and, when he was on leave, invite him to visit for ... well, that was left discreetly unspoken.

Marraines de guerre was Agence Iris's greatest success. By the end of the war, it had handled between 200,000 and 300,000 such advertisements. Amid so much correspondence, nobody noticed a dapper gentleman, always neatly dressed, or enquired why he needed three boxes to handle the replies—until they found that he used 90 different names and responded to 283 women, ten of whom disappeared shortly after. A few worried relatives reported them missing, but the police, overstretched in wartime, gave a low profile to missing persons. A shortage of men had opened the market for female bus drivers, factory workers, shop assistants and nurses. It wasn't unusual for single women to change addresses without notice.

Landru always placed the same advertisement. "Widower with two children, aged 43, with comfortable income, serious, and moving in good society, desires to meet widow with a view to matrimony." The appeal was instant. Women liked his business-like style, the promise of someone solid, reliable. And in person Landru didn't disappoint. True, he was short, and billiard-ball bald, but thick eyebrows and a flowing

Victims and the trial of Landru at Versailles, 1921

beard of deep mahogany red gave him a commanding air. He looked the model of what his victims craved; a serious man.

Shrewdly, he met his prospects in public places; railway stations, parks, particularly the Luxembourg Gardens. No out-of-the-way hotels or suburban cafés, but lawns with strolling couples, nurses with baby carriages, a brass band, and an old woman collecting payment for the use of the chairs. What could be more innocent?

Landru checked each woman in person. Some he discarded. Many he seduced. One has to admire his

systematic approach, not to mention his stamina. A
typical schedule for 19 May 1915 read:
9.30. Cigarette kiosk Gare de Lyon. Mlle. Lydie.
10.30. Café Place St. Georges, Mme. Ho.----
11.30. Metro Laundry. Mme. Le C-----
14.30. Concorde North-South. Mme. Le -----
15.30. Tour St. Jacques. Mme. Du----
17.30. Mme. Va.----
20.15. Saint Lazare. Mme. Le ----

Just as tireless in the bedroom, he passed his evenings
with a succession of these women in one of the seven city
and four suburban apartments he rented under aliases. If
one can believe sketches he made of himself while in jail,
he possessed a lengthy penis, and was expert in its use.
Most women probably never asked about his business.
To those who did, he claimed he had been in aviation
before the Germans seized his factories. If pressed, he
would describe his product, a variation on the whaling
harpoon, meant to skewer fighter planes in mid-air. (The
Air Force actually experimented with such a weapon, but
found it too heavy.)

Sometimes Landru's conquests were simply romantic,
but the 10 women he murdered, all widows, had
money, and were prepared to sign it over in return for
a respectable marriage. His modus operandi seldom
varied; a proposal, the opening of a joint bank account
into which his new fiancée deposited her savings as the
traditional *dot* or dowry; then an invitation to spend the
weekend before their wedding at his country home in
Gambais, 60 miles west of Paris. The following week,
he returned, alone, emptied the account, removed her
possessions to his warehouse, and visited Agence Iris to
clear his boxes.

The friend of a vanished widow finally recognized
Landru in the street and followed him home. Even on the

stand, he inspired belief. Cartoonists represented him as a stage magician, inviting ladies to step up from the audience and take part in his performance. He dressed so well that a wit suggested the court record note "When in town and on trial, M. Landru buys his clothes from the High Fashion Tailor." In an election that took place during his trial, he received 4000 write-in votes.

The police charged that Landru killed his victims, dismembered them, and cremated their bodies in the kitchen stove. But where was the evidence? No body ever came to light. Neighbors at Gambais talked of a stove burning late and oily black smoke streaming low over the fields. But sieving the ashes produced only 256 fragments of bone, a few metal buttons and catches of the kind used in women's corsets. Also found in the house were containers of acid that could have dissolved those parts of the corpses not burned.

Under French law, a *juge d'instruction* both leads the investigation and tries the case. A.M. Bonin, the judge assigned to Landru, had a rough ride. Grey-haired, patient and precise, a collector of art, he was no match for his puckish suspect. After Bonin laid out his case, Landru dismissed it as "a load of rubbish." Looking around the judge's office, filled with nude bronzes signed "Rodin," Landru informed him confidently that they were all fakes. (He seems to have been right. Shortly after Auguste Rodin died in 1917, the Montagutelli brothers, his plaster casters and bronze founders, were accused of making illicit copies.) He continued to mock Bonin throughout the trial, even sending him a self-portrait of himself naked, with a large erection.

Landru was caught not by forensic evidence but a simple error of thrift. As a conscientious businessman, he recorded every expense—right down to the railway tickets between Paris and the station nearest

to Gambais, Tacognieres. Reading through these records, the police saw a disparity in the case of Louise-Josephine Jaume. In June 1917, she accompanied Landru to Gambais. He had noted the costs.
Single ticket to Tacognieres—2 francs 75 centimes.
Return ticket—4 francs 40 centimes.
Why buy only a single ticket for Mme. Jaume? How was she expected to return to Paris? Landru had no answer. Convicted on all counts of murder, he was executed by guillotine at Versailles in February 1922.

LOOKING FOR LANDRU

Though Landru's house at Gambais still stands, it's a private home and there is no access. His stove, after being placed on show at the Musée Grevin, was sold to an American collector. Its present whereabouts are unknown. Executed felons were buried in the yard of the prison where the sentence was carried out. However the Museum of Death, 6031 Hollywood Blvd, Hollywood, California, displays an object that they claim to be Landru's severed head. Its provenance is obscure. Materials on the trial of Landru are on show at the Musée de la Préfecture de Police, 4, rue de la Montagne-Sainte-Geneviève (5th).

The outdoor cafés in the Luxembourg Gardens where Landru often arranged to meet his victims have not changed much in the hundred years since.

Landru's house in Gambais

CHAPTER 11

MONKEY BUSINESS: SERGE VORONOFF AND THE QUEST FOR YOUTH

Following the medical advances of World War I and research in Austria and Germany during the early 1920s, scientists began to explore the possibility of extending human life and reversing the effect of the years, compared by poet W.B. Yeats to "great black oxen [that] tread the world, And God the herdsman goads them on behind, And I am broken by their passing feet."

Noting how virility and desire decrease with age, researchers concentrated on the reproductive system. In Vienna, Eugen Steinach claimed good results by bombarding ovaries with X-rays. "We cannot perform the comic opera bouffe of transmuting an old hag into a giddy young damsel," he wrote. "But, under certain conditions, we can stretch the span of usefulness, and

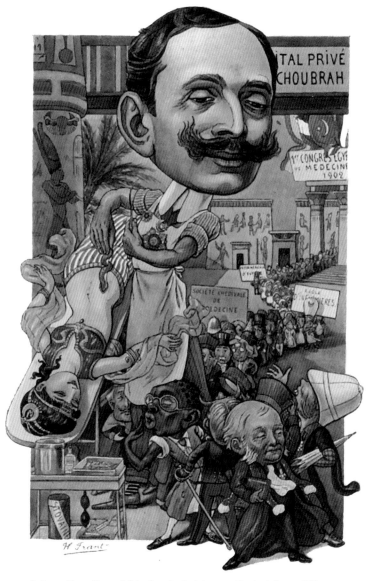

Dr. Samuel Serge Voronoff, Cairo-Romainville: Laboratory Carnine Lefrancq, 1910

enable the patient to recapture the raptures, if not the roses of youth." He promised similar good results for men by giving them vasectomies, believing that seminal fluid would back up into the system, rejuvenating it. Satirist Karl Kraus welcomed this news. Steinach, he suggested, might be able to revive the feminine in suffragettes and turn journalists into real men.

One of Steinach's patients, Californian novelist Gertrude Atherton, hailed the treatment, which returned her to "renewed mental vitality and neural energy." Working at record speed, she wrote *Black Oxen*, in which a middle-aged playwright discovers that an apparently young countess is actually a 58-year-old woman he romanced 30 years before. The countess explains that the Steinach treatment has restored 30 years of youth, with the promise of even more. "Eminent biologists who have given profound study to the subject estimate that it will last for 10 years at least, when it can be renewed." Atherton using a title from Yeats had a poetic significance, since in 1934, when he was 69, Yeats submitted to the Steinach treatment in London. To test its effectiveness, his surgeon invited him to dinner with an attractive woman, and left them alone afterwards. Yeats became a convert. "It revived my creative power," he said. "It revived also sexual desire; and that in all likelihood will last me until I die." Dublin celebrated him as "a gland old man."

As Atherton was 66 when *Black Oxen* appeared in 1923 and survived to 92, she might have appeared a living advertisement for the Steinach treatment—except that Yeats lived only another five years after his surgery. Suspicions also grew of dangerous side-effects. In 1924, the film *Vanity's Price*, from a screenplay by Paul Bern, showed a woman rejuvenated by Steinach therapy who goes insane as a result. In Conan Doyle's 1923 *The Adventure of the Creeping Man*, Sherlock

Black Oxen, 1923 and author Gertrude Atherton

Holmes investigates the erratic behavior of a professor who, about to marry a younger woman, takes pills to rejuvenate him, which instead change his personality.

By then, the center of rejuvenation therapy had shifted from Vienna to Paris, where Russian-born surgeon Serge Voronoff had arrived from Egypt to open a clinic. Voronoff, formerly personal surgeon to the Khedive or viceroy, had pioneered bone grafts and worked with distinguished physician and author Alexis Carrel. Investigating the body's rejection mechanism, he injected himself with a solution of sheep testicles, hoping it would retard aging. When it failed, he turned in 1920 to grafting minute portions of bull or monkey testicles into human scrotums. Most of his patients, some of them physicians, claimed immediate and sustained increases in energy and sexual virility. Within a decade he had treated more than 500 men, some with injections, others with transplants.

Injections or transplants from animal glands became a fad; there was even a cocktail called The Monkey

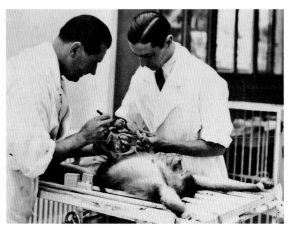

Technicians operate on a baboon giving birth at Villa Grimaldi, c. 1930

Gland. Ashtrays appeared in France showing monkeys clutching their testicles and screaming "Not me, Dr. Voronoff!" Voronoff told the American press in 1922, "already I am using four different glands from every chimpanzee received from Africa, notably thyroid glands for weak-minded children and interstitial glands for rejuvenation of the aged. The chimpanzee is the only species of monkey that can be used, it being wonderfully like a human being. The organs are identical and the bloods are indistinguishable. Chimpanzees now cost $500 each."

In California, Dr. Clayton E. Wheeler gave 12,000 goat gland injections to patients between the ages of 52 and 76. "The human body is just like a storage battery of a motor car or radio," he explained. "Its potency ebbs with use and needs to be reinvigorated at certain intervals to restore its customary vitality." In June 1922, *The New York Times* wrote, "In the last two years, the reading public has become pretty well accustomed to the almost continuous hysterical manifestations of concern for its glandular welfare. A war-ridden world has given way to a gland-ridden world. Nearly every newspaper and magazine that one picks up contains some reference—jocular or serious—to monkey glands and goat glands and the beneficent possibilities in human gland nurture and repair."

In 1923, 700 surgeons at the International Congress of Surgeons in London applauded Voronoff. Patients flocked to him, including the president of Turkey, Mustafa Kemal Atatürk. He operated three clinics around Paris, all in fashionable areas: at Villa Molière in Auteil, the Ambroise Paré nursing home in Neuilly, and on fashionable Avenue Montaigne. He also opened another in Algiers. When the French government forbade the trapping and importation of apes in 1923, he started two monkey farms to breed chimpanzees and baboons, one at Nogent-sur-Oise in the northern region of Picardie, the other in the Villa Grimaldi at Menton, which straddled the French Italian border. The mountainside estate with its giant cages became famous. Voronoff entertained numerous celebrities there, including Russian impresario Serge Diaghilev and soprano Lily Pons, who was a regular visitor.

In 1930, Einar, husband of the Paris-based illustrator Gerda Wegener, underwent the world's first sex reassignment operation in Berlin. A year later, now Lily Elbe, she submitted to further surgery to implant a uterus, which would have enabled her to have children. Instead, her body rejected the organ, and she died. Inspired by this, Voronoff transplanted a human ovary into a female monkey named Nora, and attempted to inseminate it with human sperm. That experiment also failed.

By this time, research into the male hormone testosterone was casting doubt on the methods of

Serge Voronoff (1919) and Villa Grimaldi at Menton

Steinach and Voronoff. Investigators examining
what their recipients believed were still viable grafts,
secreting hormones into their system, found only scar
tissue from the implant surgery. All primate tissue had
long since been rejected. Any supposed new potency
and energy was self-delusion.

Voronoff had already begun distancing himself. In 1939
he gave up all his research facilities in Paris and left
for a tour of the United States, Brazil and the Argentine
arranged by the Franco-Ibero-American Medical Union.
After the outbreak of war in 1939, it was no longer
prudent to return to Europe. He remained in America
until 1945, by which time the Villa Grimaldi had been
badly damaged by bombing and all his Paris clinics were
shut down.

By the time Voronoff died in 1951 at the age of 85,
few noted his passing. He was buried quietly in the
Russian section of the Caucade Cemetery in Nice.
Most physicians denied they had ever supported
him or used his methods. It was even suggested that,
in transplanting ape organs into man, he may have
unwittingly transferred the AIDS virus, though no
evidence exists to support this contention.

A few physicians remained convinced. In particular
Dr. Paul Niehans, a Swiss doctor, established a clinic to

inject animal cells into humans. His patients included Pope Pius XII, King Ibn Saoud, German President Konrad Adenauer and such film stars as Charlie Chaplin and Noel Coward. Noting that the herd of sheep used by the clinic included a single black one, Coward quipped "I see the doctor is expecting [African-American singer] Paul Robeson."

THE MONKEY IN THE MIDDLE

Gertrude Atherton was not the last person to see the dramatic possibilities of rejuvenation. H.G. Wells's 1896 novel *The Island of Doctor Moreau* takes place on a Pacific island where a doctor uses surgery to create creatures that are part animal and part man.

Voronoff's apparent success, combined with the popularity of such novels as Edgar Rice Burroughs' *Tarzan of the Apes*, in which an English orphan is raised by monkeys, fed the fantasy that apes and men could socialize, and even interbreed. In 1930, novelist Félicien Champsaur wrote *Ouha, Roi des Singes*, (*Ouha, King of Apes*). In it, an American scientist educates an exceptionally intelligent monkey from Borneo to become "the Napoleon of Apes," only to see him destroyed when he falls in love with the scientist's daughter, a prefiguring of *King Kong*. Champsaur followed with *Nora, la guenon devenue femme* (*Nora, the Monkey Turned Woman*). Suggested by Voronoff's experiment of ovary transplant but directly inspired by the arrival on the Paris stage of part-African American performer Joséphine Baker. In a racist speculation typical of the era, it proposed that Nora did produce a daughter, a combination of human and ape that grew into Baker.

CHAPTER 12

FARAWAY PLACES: THE BIRTH OF TOURISM

As international visitors flooded into France, eager for the metropolitan experience, European travelers, particularly the French, looked with new interest towards those regions of Asia and Africa that remained relatively unexplored.

Influenced by the 18th-century philosopher Jean-Jacques Rousseau, who suggested that the "savages" of Africa and the Pacific were actually "natural men," blessedly free of the burdens of civilization, fashionable Paris was swept with a vogue for artifacts from France's Indochinese and North African colonies. Expat publisher/poet Nancy Cunard ringed her slim arms with tribal bracelets of carved wood and hammered metal while Man Ray juxtaposed the face of his model and mistress Alice Prin, aka Kiki of Montparnasse, with a Senegalese mask. Benin bronzes impressed Pablo Picasso, Guillaume Apollinaire and Georges Braque

La Croisière Noire, 1924

La Croisière Noire, cinema poster

with their purity of form. Reflecting this interest, and following the lead of Napoleon I who took artists and writers with him when he invaded Egypt, ethnographic expeditions of the 1920s recruited painters, photographers, writers, and, increasingly, filmmakers.

Central to this urge to explore was André Citroën, France's leading automobile manufacturer. One of his engineers, Adolphe Kégresse, had perfected an auto-chenille or caterpillar car whose rear wheels ran on a tank-like half-track. To demonstrate its capabilities, Citroën organized a *raid* or expedition across Africa. Beginning in October 1924 in Colomb-Béchar, Algeria, the eight cars crossed the Sahara—the first automobiles to do so—and ploughed through equatorial jungles before separating. One team crossed to the island of Madagascar while the other headed for the Cape of Good Hope. Among the 17 team members were a film crew and a painter, ensuring the journey was meticulously documented.

For Citroën, this *Croisière Noire* or Black Expedition was a publicity triumph, particularly after the feature-length documentary film opened in Paris. The journey advertised Citroën automobiles but also opened up new overland routes, with resulting political and economic gains. Much credit for its success went to Georges-Marie Haardt, Citroën's general manager, whom he placed in command. The backbone of the expedition, Haardt was a hard taskmaster. Even in the desert, each man was required to dress correctly and shave every day.

Not all expeditions were so well-ordered. In Southeast Asia, such adventurers as the young André Malraux, later a prominent novelist, filmmaker and politician who served as Charles DeGaulle's minister of culture, were looting Cambodian temple sculptures for sale to eager museum curators and private collectors. Arrested in 1923, Malraux blamed his detention on corrupt French

André Citroën

authorities who resented an amateur horning in on their lucrative business.

Author André Gide made two visits to the Congo and Chad in 1925 and 1926. Instead of Rousseau's "natural man," he found tribal people cruelly oppressed and exploited. His books about the trips bitterly criticized colonialism, particularly in the Congo, which was still cringing from the brutality of its former oppressors, the Belgians.

Following the *Croisière Noire*, Citroën and Haardt mounted an Asian journey, the *Croisière Jaune* or Yellow Expedition. One team would set out east from Beirut, crossing the Soviet Union, while another, starting from Beijing and heading west, would traverse the Gobi Desert, the two meeting somewhere in central Asia.

From the start in April 1931, nothing went well. The China team, joined by Jesuit priest and religious philosopher Teilhard de Chardin, was held for several months in Urumqi, capital of Sinkiang, by a warlord who envied their half-tracks. To ransom the team, Citroën had to send two new vehicles from Paris.

The eastward group, denied permission to enter the Soviet Union, headed into Kashmir and crossed the Himalayas—an extraordinary feat, during which the cars had to be disassembled and hand-carried over mountain passes. Crossing a frozen storm-swept Gobi desert sapped what remained of the expedition's strength. Though the raid concluded triumphantly in Paris in February 1932, Georges-Marie Haardt wasn't present. He had collapsed from exhaustion and died in Hong Kong, en route to Europe.

Tragedy continued to haunt the expedition when one of the team, Lieutenant Victor Point, learned on his return

Crossing the Himalaya, La Croisière Jaune, 1931

that his fiancée, actress Alice Cocéa, had taken another lover in his absence. On holiday with her on the Riviera, he took her out in a small boat and shot himself in front of her. Cocéa was starring in a Paris musical but furious audiences disrupted her performances, chanting "*Point! Point! Point!*" until she announced she was leaving show business to enter a convent.

Once again, the documentary film of the expedition aroused public imagination. Despite financial difficulties, Citroën began planning the *Croisière Blanche*, a White Expedition to promote his cars in the Americas. This time the half-tracks would cross northern Canada from Edmonton to the Pacific, traversing the Rocky Mountains.

Meanwhile, expeditions for Africa and Asia left Paris almost monthly, often with as many artists on the staff as scientists. Surrealist poet Michel Leiris signed on as archivist with a Dakar-Djibouti Expedition, which sailed from Bordeaux in May 1931. Also on board were an ethnomusicologist, a naturalist, and a painter. Finding Rousseau's "natural man" wasn't high on its agenda. In his book about the journey, *L'Afrique fantôme* (*Phantom Africa*), Leiris, nostalgic for Paris, marveled at how little affinity he felt for Africans. "Do you know," he wrote a friend, "I haven't had sex with even one African woman. That's how little I've changed."

No less eager than the explorers to realize on the value of its colonial possessions, the French government mounted the 1931 *Exposition Coloniale Internationale* to encourage investment and exports. It occupied most of the Bois de Vincennes, a park on the edge of Paris. More than 20 French colonies in Africa, Indochina and the Pacific, as well as possessions of other European powers, were represented by often lavish pavilions or whole settlements, including a reconstruction of part of Angkor Wat in Cambodia, ironically one of the sites most despoiled by treasure hunters. Restaurants served ethnic food, and tribal people demonstrated their ceremonies and ways of life. At the same time, the government constructed on the site a striking new museum in Art Déco style, the *Musée Nationale des Arts d'Afrique et d'Océanie*.

Citroën's decision with his *Croisière Blanche* to leave Africa and Asia for North America brought disaster. Under the command of Charles Bedaux, a flamboyant character who had already crossed Africa from east to west and driven across Tibet, the party, which included both Bedaux's wife and mistress, left Edmonton in five vehicles in July 1934. But half-tracks that had defeated the Himalayas were no match for the Rockies, particularly without the steadying hand of Georges-Marie Haardt. Overwhelmed by rainstorms, the expedition lost three cars in mudslides, and abandoned the remaining two.

André Citroën, bankrupt, died in 1935. His dream of a network of international highways crowded with Citroën automobiles would not be realized in his lifetime. The 33 million visitors to the Colonial Exposition took away with them the news that Africa was ripe for exploitation. At the same time, enthusiasm waned for the image of Africa and Asia as repositories of native wisdom. As this high-minded impulse faded, exploration by default was left to the looters.

The Dakar-Djibouti expedition, of which Michael Leiris was a part, would become the most highly publicized of all *raids*. Dazzled by the richness of Africa's art objects, it plundered indiscriminately. On its return, leader Marcel Griaule presented Paris's Musée d'Ethnographie with his "sumptuous booty," 3600 items of sculpture or craftwork, 6000 photographs, 1600 meters of film and 1500 pages of documentation. There was more than enough to stock a new Musée de l'Homme or Museum of Man, filling a wing of the Palais de Chaillot, on the hill of the Trocadero overlooking the Tour Eiffel. Its first exhibition opened on June 2, 1933. Significantly, the guest of honor was not a distinguished ethnographer but African-American music-hall and movie star Joséphine Baker. She flirted and jived among the exhibits, to the delight of the press and the newsreel cameras.

Paradoxically, the presence of so much tribal art in Paris revived an appreciation of the folkways of France itself. The expansion of railroads and autoroutes made every corner of the nation accessible. The 1930s saw a new interest in local history, customs, costume and language. Like Wales, Scotland and Ireland in Great Britain, the French regions of Brittany, Corsica and Alsace asserted political ambitions. Breton French revived as a living language, and Corsican separatists would soon be campaigning vigorously, even violently, for self-government.

CHAPTER 13

FASTER, HIGHER, STRONGER, MEANER: THE 1924 OLYMPIC GAMES

But for a film sequence of barefoot young athletes running in slow motion along a beach to the music of Vangelis, few people would know or care about the 1924 Olympic Games in Paris. But in dramatizing the events behind the running of the 100 meters final, Hugh Hudson's 1981 movie *Chariots of Fire* cast a tantalizing sideways light on the social, political, nationalist, financial and religious forces that would come to dominate sports.

After the disastrous 1900 Olympiad in Paris, marred by squabbling among rival ruling bodies, flagrant cheating, and an eccentric selection of sports (balloon racing; croquet; pigeon shooting with live pigeons), Baron Pierre de Coubertin hoped the 1924 games, his

Eric Liddell is paraded around Edinburgh University after winning the 400 metres at the 1924 Paris Olympics.

Eric Liddell winning gold at the 1924 Olympics

last, would dignify the movement he launched. Though Amsterdam had already been chosen over Barcelona, Los Angeles, Rome and Prague to play host, the Baron, about to step down from leadership, pleaded that Paris deserved a chance to redeem the 1900 debacle.

In practice, the events of 1924 came close to eclipsing it.

Foreshadowing the political agendas that would lead to the 1980 U.S. boycott of the Moscow games and the U.S.S.R.'s reciprocal withdrawal from Los Angeles in 1984, the American government used the 1924 Olympics to play politics. On the eve of the games, the United States strongly censured France for having invaded Germany's rich industrial Ruhr area in an effort to extract unpaid war reparations. Paris crowds cursed and spat on American athletes. Ironically, the country at the center of the controversy, Germany, was not invited to compete.

America's rugby footballers suffered particularly violent abuse. Included for the first time in the games, rugby promised an easy gold medal for France, a world leader in the sport. The U.S. team, after being initially refused admission to France, then denied practice space, insulted in the press, and robbed of money and valuables, met France on May 18th in what was manifestly a grudge match. After French star Adolphe Jaureguy was carried off unconscious with a broken nose, local fans turned on American spectators in the crowd and beat them senseless, then watched stone-faced as their limp, bloodied bodies were passed over their heads to ambulances on the field. When the visitors won 17-3, French supporters rioted. Had police not erected new metal fences in expectation of trouble, the Americans might not have survived. As it was, the roar of protest and abuse was so great that it drowned out the playing of the U.S. national anthem during the award ceremony.

A quieter revolution was taking place in the British athletic team. Harold Abrahams and Eric Liddell were rivals in the 100 meters until Liddell learned that the final would be run on a Sunday. A devout Christian who later became a missionary in China, he refused to compete on the Sabbath. Withdrawing from the 100 meters before the Games, he began retraining for the 400 meters. Abrahams won the 100 meters, but Liddell, against all expectations, took the 400 meters in world-record time.

Britain also figured in a boxing scandal. Harry Mallin, defending middleweight champion, met Frenchman Roger Brousse in the quarter-finals. As the bout ended, Mallin protested to the referee that Brousse had repeatedly bitten him. He was ignored, and the decision awarded to Brousse on points. However, when Argentina's Manolo Gallardo also complained of being bitten, a Swedish official demanded an inquiry. Brousse claimed he snapped his teeth together when he threw a

The 1924 Olympic poster

punch, and that Mallin and Gallardo had simply bumped him at the wrong time. The jury decided the Frenchman didn't bite intentionally, but still disqualified him. At the final bout two days later, Brousse, wearing gloves and trunks, appeared with a mob of fans who, in the midst of uproar, boosted him into the ring with Mallin and his opponent. Police had to be called to remove Brousse and his supporters. Mallin went on to win.

When de Coubertin revived the Olympic Games in 1896, he included a medal for mountain climbing. It was awarded for the first and last time in 1924, to the members of a 1922 British team that had attempted to scale Mount Everest. They came within 500 meters of the summit, but failed three times to reach it. Britain mounted another expedition in 1924. A member, Lieutenant Colonel Edward Strutt, came to Chamonix to accept 13 silver-gilt medals, one for each British member of the party. He pledged that, if possible, one would be placed on the summit. Unfortunately the expedition not only failed to conquer the mountain; seven Sherpa porters died in an avalanche. The Olympic body hastily minted eight more medals, and presented them to the one surviving Nepalese and the grieving families of the others. Strutt's pledge wasn't honored until 2012, when a team financed by the electronics giant Samsung placed one of the medals on the peak.

The 1924 games did produce some notable victories. Johnny Weissmuller, later Hollywood's Tarzan, took three gold medals in swimming, and Benjamin Spock, destined to write some classic works on child care, rowed in the triumphant eights crew. In the final medal tally, the United States led with 45 gold, followed by tiny Finland with 38. The host nation, France, trailed humiliatingly with 37, though well ahead of Britain's nine.

Finland owed its triumph to one man, distance runner Paavo Nurmi. Known as The Flying Finn, he put on an exhibition of disciplined physical achievement that not only won personal gold but inspired his national team to victory. Running with a stopwatch on his wrist, Nurmi won the 1,500 and 5,000-meter finals within an hour of each other, and set Olympic records in both. Two days later, he won the 10,000-meter cross-country run after a tough course and blistering heat caused 23 of the 38 starters to drop out.

Johnny Weissmuller won three Olympic gold medals in 1924 and enjoyed a successful acting career as *Tarzan*

Nurmi's sportsmanship shamed the cheats who dominated the 1924 games. The Olympiad concluded with many believing there would never be another. Aside from the numerous abuses, it was a financial disaster, earning only 5.5 million francs of the 10 million francs it cost. The *Times of London* called its report "the funeral oration of the Olympic Games; not of these particular Games only but of the whole Olympic movement." It continued "The ideal which inspired the re-birth of the Games was a high one—namely by friendly rivalry and sport to bind together the youth of all nations in a brotherhood so close and long that it would form a bulwark against the outbreak of all international animosities. But the world is not yet ripe for such a brotherhood." That the Olympic movement survived not only the scandals of 1924 and such politically motivated games as those staged in Berlin in 1936 but also repeated cases of corruption and incompetence within its own ranks is proof, if not of international brotherhood, then of the enduring and passionate desire of mankind to watch others strive, in the motto of the Games, to be "faster, higher, stronger."

SEE IT: WHERE THE GAMES TOOK PLACE

Because of a shortage of venues, events were more widely dispersed in 1924 than in modern Olympiads. Sailing took place on the English Channel at Le Havre and clay target shooting at the satellite town of Issy-les-Moulineaux. The primary venue was the Stade Olympique in Colombes, 10 kilometers north-west of central Paris. It hosted the athletics, certain cycling and equestrian events, all the gymnastics and tennis, some of the football and rugby, and the running and fencing heats of the modern pentathlon. The stadium still stands, although many features, including its concrete grandstands, have been demolished for safety reasons, reducing its original 45,000-person capacity to about 14,000.

Two other 1924 venues were also demolished: the Stade Bergeyre near Parc des Buttes Chaumont, site of some rugby matches, and the Velodrome d'Hiver or winter bicycle track, a covered auditorium used for boxing, fencing, weight-lifting and wrestling events. The "Vel d'Hiv" stood at the corner of rue Nélaton (15th). It became notorious during World War II when French police imprisoned Jews there awaiting deportation. The building burned in 1959. A plaque marks the site.

CHAPTER 14

"LITTLE GIRL, CAN YOU DO THE CHARLESTON?": LE JAZZ HOT

What Paris in the 1920s called "jazz" referred less to the music than to a culture that encompassed Americanized stage revues and nightclubs, the newest U.S. fashions in clothing and hairstyles, Hollywood movies, and the geometric, stylized form of decoration later labeled "Art Déco." The music to which some danced and which acted as an obbligato to the prevailing wildness was called, in an early example of the pidgin known as Franglais, "le jazz hot."

Most French audiences first heard authentic Afro-American jazz during World War I when the band of James Reese Europe toured to entertain the troops. Former musical director to dancers Vernon and Irene Castle, Europe, a lieutenant in the National Guard, was

Joséphine Baker dancing the Charleston at the Folies Bergère, 1926

both a gifted, highly-educated musician and a natural leader. His 65-member unit comprised singers, dancers and comedians, as well as such jazz celebrities as Buddy Gilmore, regarded as the first modern jazz drummer, cornetist Noble Sissle, and dancer Bill "Bojangles" Robinson. Had he returned to France after the war, Europe might have become an important ecumenical force in Franco-American music. However, in 1919 he was stabbed and killed trying to stop a brawl between two jealous drummers.

Europe's musicians could all read music, but as American audiences preferred the illusion of spontaneity in what was then called "race music," his sidemen memorized their often intricate arrangements. Paradoxically this convinced the French that jazz was a skill unique to black Americans. For whites to attempt it was regarded as unwise, even unnatural. Leonid Massine, choreographing the 1917 Erik Satie/ Jean Cocteau ballet *Parade*, caused a sensation by incorporating dances seen previously only in visiting all-black minstrel shows. Particularly scandalous was his use of the one-step, which James Reese Europe claimed to have invented, and which he called "the national dance of the Negro." Sharing the general shock, young composer Francis Poulenc wrote "For the first time, music hall was invading art-with-a-Capital-A. A one-step is danced in *Parade*! When that began, the audience let loose with boos and applause."

The belief that only African-Americans could play jazz acted as a gilt-edged invitation to black musicians to perform in Europe. The moment they were demobilized, many headed back to the country where their expertise was valued, even revered, and where, moreover, they experienced none of the racial prejudice endemic in the United States. Among them, a band formed by James Reese Europe's former sideman Noble Sissle toured

Ada "Bricktop" Smith, 1934

extensively in France and Germany.

The arrival in Paris of black musicians coincided with an influx of tourists who, particularly after the imposition of Prohibition in 1920, flooded its bars, restaurants and brothels, demanding cocktails and entertainment. Tiny clubs sprang up on the lower slopes of Montmartre, along such streets as rue Pigalle and rue Fontaine, already notorious as hangouts for prostitutes. For any club that expected to attract foreign clientele, a *bar Americaine* with a black bartender and a jazz band, entirely African-American, were indispensable.

Black entrepreneurs ran many of these clubs, or at least fronted them for local businessmen. In 1924, Eugene Bullard, the only African-American air ace, opened Le Grand Duc on rue Pigalle. One of his waiters was the later-famous Harlem poet Langston Hughes. Ada Smith, a dancer from New York whose red hair indicated her mixed-race parentage, became famous as a protégée of song writer Cole Porter, who had sat out the war studying music at Paris's Schola Cantorum. Spotting the red-headed Ada, he asked "Little girl, can you do the

Poster for *La Revue Negre* at the Champs Elysees, Paul Colin, 1925

Charleston?" When she demonstrated vigorously, Porter
exclaimed, "What legs! What legs!" He nicknamed her
"Bricktop," and feted her so often at his parties that she
opened her own club, Chez Bricktop, soon to become the
most famous in Paris. In tribute, Porter wrote the blues-
like "Miss Otis Regrets" specifically for Smith to perform.

In 1925, painter Fernand Léger suggested to his friend,
the impresario André Daven, that an all-black American

revue might fill the enormous Theatre de Champs-Elysées as the Ballets Russes had done before the war. Daven hired Caroline Dudley Reagan in New York to put together a company of 28, including twelve musicians, among them the soprano saxophonist Sidney Bechet, and eight dancers, one of whom was Joséphine Baker. From her first appearance on the Paris stage, naked except for a large feather and draped over the shoulder of a husky young man, also mostly nude, Baker who, like Bricktop, was of mixed-race parentage, became, for the Parisian audience, synonymous with jazz. When the company returned to the United States, she stayed in France. After becoming a star at the Folies Bergère, she too opened a club in Montmartre. Sidney Bechet also returned in 1928 and led a small band at Chez Bricktop, but was deported after his involvement in a gunfight.

As young French musicians grappled with the intricacies of a musical form that apparently could not be taught, since almost nothing was written down, composers of the avant garde, in particular the group known as Les Six, experimented with African and Caribbean music, hoping to find a new route into this enigmatic music. One of the group, Darius Milhaud, after a visit to Brazil, wrote "*Le Bœuf sur le toit,*" literally "*The Bull on the Roof,*" the title of a Brazilian folk song. Jean Cocteau, with the Fratellini clown brothers, created a ballet to the music, and club owner Louis Moysès adopted it as the name for his new bar. Shortly after, "*bœuf*" entered the language as slang for a jam session.

In 1918, another of Les Six, Francis Poulenc, premiered "La Rapsodie nègre," in which a baritone sang words supposedly written by "Liberian poet Makoko Kangourou." The name was as false as the text, which included such lines as "Honoloulou, poti lama! / honoloulou, honoloulou, / kati moko, mosi bolou." Poulenc probably mirrored the American poet Vachel

Lindsay and his 1914 poem "The Congo," which also contains examples of nonsense African dialect, e.g. "boomlay boomlay boomlay boom... Mumbo-jumbo will hoo-doo you." Lindsay declaimed his poems from a stage, hoping, as Poulenc did, to achieve the effect of jazz improvisation. Both failed, since neither understood the musical language they tried to emulate.

African-American musicians continued to relocate in Paris, and revues to tour. The most massive, the hundred-strong Lew Leslie's Black Birds, starring singer Adelaide Hall and featuring the Jazz Plantation Orchestra, arrived in June 1929 and filled Paris's 1500-seat Moulin Rouge, one of Europe's largest theatres. Its songs, including "I Can't Give You Anything but Love, Baby," "Diga Diga Do," and "I Must Have That Man," were already widely known from records, but audiences flocked to hear *le jazz hot* at white heat. Joseph Wechsberg, one of the local musicians hired to augment the band, lamented "Our feeble attempts were drowned by the ear-splitting racket of 50 saxophones, clarinets, trombones, trumpets, banjos, helicon horns, pianos and drums."

Black Birds marked the high point of Franco/American jazz relations. During the Depression, impresarios went broke and clubs closed. By the time prosperity returned, Paris was less interested in jazz and tourists no longer so ready to spend time and money there. "The formidable political challenges facing France and central Europe had begun to mute the clamor and hilarity of Montmartre's nightly street life," wrote jazz historian William Shack. "By April 1938, the two principal streets of Montmartre for black cabaret life, rue Pigalle and rue Fontaine, were bare and nearly deserted."

The hiatus of the early 1930s gave French players a breathing space to experiment more with jazz.

La Boule Blanche, Brassaï, 1932

Significantly, the European popular music closest
in spirit was Romany or gypsy music, from which
France's one authentic jazz master appeared. Unable
to read either words or music, Django Reinhardt had
fewer hurdles to surmount in understanding the new
music. Listening to recordings of the Duke Ellington
band, guitarist Eddie Lang and violinist Joe Venuti, he
developed an easy-going, laid-back, often dreamy style
of jazz that, while echoing such early American players
as cornetist Bix Biederbecke, achieved a uniquely
European tone.

Les Six and Jean Cocteau, 1931

In 1932, a group of musicians and intellectuals formed the Hot Club of France to stage concerts with local jazz men. At one of them, Reinhardt played for the first time with violinist Stéphane Grappelli. Delighted at the synergy, the Hot Club formed the Quintet of the Hot Club of France, featuring Reinhardt and Grappelli, and arranged for them to be recorded and to go on tour. Although the fastidious Grappelli came to detest the hard-drinking, free-spending and irresponsible Reinhardt, the music they created was unequalled. French musicians searching for the secret of *le jazz hot* had been looking in the wrong places; what Reinhardt and Grappelli achieved was something more rare and more French: *le jazz frais*—a jazz not hot but cool.

MEMORIES OF *LE JAZZ HOT*

Paris has few memorials to those individuals of the 1920s and 30s who epitomized *le jazz hot*. Joséphine Baker is commemorated twice: by a small square in Montparnasse, Place Joséphine Baker, near the theater street of rue de la Gaite (14th), and, rather more puzzlingly, by a public swimming pool at the Porte de la Gare (13th). Reflecting the help given to her at the end of her life by Princess Grace, she is buried in Monaco. Her club, Chez Joséphine, was at 40, rue Fontaine (9th). Ada Smith operated various clubs as Chez Bricktop, one of them at 66, rue Pigalle, now rue Jean-Baptiste Pigalle: the building was demolished in 2004. Eugene Bullard's Le Grand Duc was at 52, rue Jean-Baptiste Pigalle. The first Bœuf Sur le Toit began in 1922 in an 18th-century building at 28, rue Boissy d'Anglas. It later transferred to Nos. 21, 28 and 33 in the same street. In 1941, it moved up-market to chic Art Déco premises at 34, rue du Colisée (all addresses 8th). The present restaurant displays souvenirs of Cocteau and the café's previous incarnations. There is a resident jazz group, with singer, and occasional visiting musicians preserve the tradition of the *boeuf*. Although it deals with a period after World War II, Bertrand Tavernier's 1986 film *'Round Midnight*, the story of a broken-down jazzman befriended by a young French fan (and based on the friendship of pianist Bud Powell and Francis Paudras), remains the most accurate depiction on film of the French love affair with American music.

LES ANNÉES FOLLES

Clockwise from top left: Repainting of the Eiffel Tower, 1924; The Hoffman Girls at dressing room of Moulin Rouge, 1924; Le Monocle, a special cabaret for women in Montparnasse, 1930; Louise Brooks Studio-publicity still for *Rolled Stockings*, c. 1927; a Christmas Eve at Maxim's Paris, 1925

Clockwise from top : Bal musette "La Java", 1925; Fernand Léger on the set of *L'inhumaine* directed by Marcel L'Herbier, 1924; Edith Piaf in Paris, c. 1930; Three women (prostitutes) in a doorway on rue Asselin, Eugène Atget, 1924-25

CHAPTER 15

ARTIFICIAL PARADISES: ABSINTHE, OPIUM, AND THE CULTURE OF FORGETTING

For anyone wishing to get drunk or stoned during the years between the wars, there was no better place than Paris. "The 1914-1918 war made everyone drunk," Gertrude Stein wrote. "There was never so much drunkenness in France as there was then, soldiers all learned to drink, everybody drank." France's vineyards produced the world's best wine and the regions of Cognac and Armagnac the best brandies. The brewing of absinthe, distilled from the drug wormwood and tinted green with herbs and fennel, was a national industry.

Opium den, Brassaï, 1931

Opium smoking from the French film, *Dandy-Pacha*, 1918

With the poppy fields of its Indochinese colonies and the cannabis plantations of Algeria and Morocco, France also dominated the market in opium and hashish. In 1860, Charles Baudelaire coined the term "artificial paradises" to celebrate the altered states of consciousness offered by drugs. "Common sense tells us that the things of the earth exist only a little," he wrote, "and that true reality is only in dreams." And the road to dreams led through the bowl of a pipe.

Until the 1930s, Europe only casually monitored the sale of drugs. Although aspirin, as a synthetic, was available only by prescription, cocaine, heroin, opium and cannabis, all "natural" plant compounds, could be bought at any pharmacy as pills, gels, syrups, even teas. During the *belle époque*, morphine was the fashionable drug of choice. Military officers and their mistresses carried the most popular hypodermic, the Pravaz, which could be custom-made in precious metals and decorated with jewels as a gift.

During World War I, Harrods, London's most select department store, possessors of the Royal Warrant to supply goods to the king and queen, sold phials of heroin gel, and a drug kit containing cocaine, morphine, syringes and needles, which it recommended to "sweethearts and mothers" as "a Welcome Present for Friends at the Front." The government reluctantly restricted its sale when commanders complained of officers too stoned to go "over the top."

In the same way, the French only intervened to ban absinthe in 1914 when it was feared it might sap the ability of young Frenchmen to fight. Ironically, troops had once been issued with absinthe during the 19th century as a supposed preventive for malaria. Correctly distilled, it was perfectly safe; the damage was done by home-distillation, which failed to remove the alkaloid, thujone, responsible for brain damage and blindness.

The ban didn't upset troops in the trenches. They were not particularly partial to absinthe, which needed to be mixed with water and sugar for its best effect. Rough red wine, called *pinard*, was their preferred drink. A postcard intended for circulation strictly among the troops showed an old soldier clutching six looted bottles of *pinard*. "With this," he grins, "we'll give them a good hosing."

Each *poilu* or common soldier carried two one-liter *bidons* or canteens. One generally held water mixed with *pinard*. The second contained tafia, a cheap rum from Haiti, distilled from molasses after the sugar has been extracted.

Quality rum was aged in wooden casks to improve the flavor and disperse such poisons as fusel oil. In the process, it lost some of its alcohol. Tafia, sold straight from the still, retained all the impurities, as well as a ferociously high alcohol content: in most cases 100 proof—60 percent alcohol. The test of potency was

Parisian absinthe poster, 1890

simple. One mixed tafia with gunpowder and lit a match. The good stuff exploded. Officers not only encouraged drinking tafia before an attack but sometimes doled out what they called *un gout de rendre fou*—a drop to make you crazy. African-American Eugene Bullard, fighting in the Foreign Legion, agreed. "It made us more like madmen than soldiers."

The 19th century had introduced man to only one entirely new sensation—speed. Its necessary antithesis was opium, one special quality of which was to numb the sense of time. As long as one continued to drag its smoke into your lungs, time ceased to exist. It also killed the appetite for both food and sex—a small price to pay for its other pleasures. "Everything one does in life, even love, occurs in an express train racing toward death," wrote Jean Cocteau. "To smoke opium is to escape from the train while it is still moving. It is to concern oneself with something other than life or death."

When Hungarian photographer Gyula Halasz, aka Brassai, visited an opium den or *fumerie* in the 1930s, he asked to photograph one of its clients, a beautiful actress. "Of course!" she said. "I'm proud to smoke. They say that after a while opium will make you thin, weaken you, ruin your mind, your memory. Rot! Look at me, and tell me frankly, am I not beautiful and desirable? I've smoked opium for ten years and I'm doing all right." Since one couldn't eat while under its influence, opium would have helped that actress by controlling her weight.

But while not as powerful as its refined variants, morphine, heroin and codeine, opium was addictive. Many women were hooked on laudanum, a solution of opium dissolved in spiced alcohol. The Prozac of its day, it was widely used, and abused. Jean Cocteau, who sometimes smoked up to 60 pipes a day, periodically entered a clinic to kick the habit, though it soon returned.

Fumeries, like brothels, came in all forms in Paris. Expatriates preferred Drosso's. For Caresse Crosby, it was "the one place in Paris where the sumptuous rapture of the east was evoked in the ease and luxury of the surroundings." On arrival, clients exchanged their clothes for silk kimonos. After that, explained Crosby, "we stepped in upon a scene from the Arabian Nights. The apartment was a series of small fantastic rooms, large satin divans heaped with pillows, walls covered with gold-embroidered arras, in the centre of each room a low round stand on which was ranged all the paraphernalia of the pipe. By the side of each table, in coolie dress, squatted a little servant of the lamp. The air was sweet with the smell of opium." For important clients, Drosso, dressed in a kimono decorated with a giant butterfly, prepared the pipes himself. "The soft clouds wooed one's body," wrote Caresse, "winding and unwinding its spell, holding one in a web of lustless rapture. Smiling, one relaxed and drowsed, another's arms around one, it mattered little whose."

For those who preferred more privacy when they smoked, dealers like Drosso would arrange an opium party in one's home. As well as the drug and all the equipment, they provided *congees* or servants who prepared pipes, kept smokers comfortable while they were under the influence, and provided sexual favors to any guests not partaking of the drug.

North Africans preferred hashish, the gum of the cannabis plant. It could be smoked, sniffed, and eaten, sometimes in confectionery. When Alice B. Toklas, companion of Gertrude Stein, compiled *The Alice B. Toklas Cookbook* in 1954, she asked former guests to recall their favorite dishes. Bryon Gysin, companion of writer William S. Burroughs, sent a recipe for a mixture of honey, nuts, dried fruits, spices and cannabis. "It might provide an entertaining refreshment for a Ladies' Bridge Club," wrote Gysin, tongue in cheek. "In Morocco it is thought to be good for warding off the common cold in damp winter weather and is, indeed, more effective if taken with quantities of hot mint tea. Euphoria and brilliant storms of laughter; ecstatic reveries and extensions of one's personality on several simultaneous planes are to be complacently expected." Whether she failed to get the joke or recognized it but played along anyway, she included the recipe, along with Gysin's commentary, thus launching a tradition of using cannabis in cakes and brownies that persists to this day.

SEE IT: BUT DON'T SMOKE IT — OPIUM AND ABSINTHE ARTIFACTS

Though opium use is illegal in modern France, the tradition is celebrated at the Musée du Fumeur, 7, rue Pache (11th) by a display of pipes and other opium memorabilia. There are additional opium-related items in the Musée des Arts Decoratifs, 107-109 rue de Rivoli (3rd), the Musée Carnavalet, 23, rue de Sevigne (4th), Bibliothèque Forney, 1, rue du Figuer (5th) and many other institutes of ethnographic and Asiatic studies. Pipes and other opium-iana turn up occasionally in antique shops and street markets, as well as the pierced spoons and special glasses used for the correct serving of absinthe. Some Paris bars specialize in absinthe, notably La Fée Verte, 108, rue de la Roquette, (11th), which offers a range of absinthes and the correct equipment for serving. The apartment occupied by Gertrude Stein and Alice B. Toklas at 27, rue de Fleurus (6th) is not open to the public but a plaque on the wall indicates its location. Brian Gysin's recipe for Hashish Fudge was dropped from the first British edition of *The Alice B. Toklas Cook Book*, but appears in most later printings.

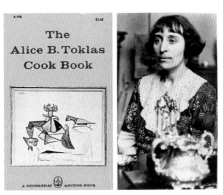

The Alice B. Toklas Cook Book, 1954 and Alice B. Toklas, 1922

CHAPTER 16

IN THE WHITE CITY: THE BIRTH OF ART DÉCO

Rarely has the cover of a book conveyed so vividly the function for which it's intended. Against a gold background, a stylized green man lifts a glass to his lips. A jagged silver lightning bolt leaps from the glass to his heart. A panel down the outer edge explodes in an avalanche of silver, black and gold. Pow!

After such an illustration, the title—*The Savoy Cocktail Book*—comes as an anticlimax. Of course, it's about alcohol. This is 1930, and the cocktail—in its celebration of variety, its concern for style over function, its striving for instant effect—has become the sign in which the 20th century conquers. From the cover of this recipe book of booze, the jazz age shouts at the only volume it knows—*fortissimo*—and in its visual language of choice, Art Déco.

Grand Salon of the Hôtel d'un Collectionneur, Emile-Jacques Ruhlmann, 1925

The Savoy Cocktail Book and Exposition des Arts Décoratifs Paris 1925

Throughout the spring and summer of 1925, a new white city grew along the banks of the Seine. The largest buildings of that area, the 17th-century Hôtel des Invalides and the massive Grand Palais, built in 1900, were outshone, literally, by scores of low white plaster "pavilions," many as fancifully detailed as wedding cakes in silver and gold. A British visitor called it "a Cubist dream city, or the projection of a possible city on Mars."

Paris specialized in international exhibitions. The layout of the city, with its numerous parks and open spaces along the Seine, made it ideal for such shows, and they had proved a spectacular success in promoting exports. But the Exposition Internationale des Arts Decoratifs Modernes of 1925 was something new. Intended as a rebuke to a Germany increasingly aggressive in the world of design, it would be a reminder to the world that French art and workmanship remained supreme.

However, in presenting a summary of everything artistically original developed in France since the end of World War I, the organizers faced a problem. There was no agreement among artists of what constituted a truly modern style. While they admired the slickness and machine finish of automobiles, aircraft and motorcycles, and the functionalism and avoidance of decoration that was already appearing in such personal accessories as cameras, wristwatches, cigarette cases and lighters, they were loath to discard entirely the femininity of prewar Art Nouveau, which adapted well to almost every use of design from architecture to jewelry.

Surprisingly for a nation not known for consensus, the design community took relatively little time to agree. Essentially, they compromised on the classicism in which all of them had been educated, and for which the French public since the time of Napoleon I had showed such affection. The new synthesis of classicism and modernism became so instantly recognizable that nobody named it. Not until the 1960s would scholars agree on the title "Art Déco."

An architect from ancient Greece touring the 1925 Exposition would have felt right at home. The smooth cylindrical columns of many pavilions would have been familiar, even though they lacked the classical bases and capitals. He would have approved the many fountains, gardens, courtyards, decorative friezes and statuary groups, while wondering, not being acquainted with Modigliani and the Cubists, at the way figures were elongated and stylized.

Unlike earlier trade expositions at which the state had been the main exhibitor, there were no massive halls crammed with examples of the national imagination. The Grande Palais housed a range of work from the most distinguished of contemporary designers. Otherwise, pavilions were sponsored by department stores or individual manufacturers, both French and foreign, interspersed with those of guest nations.

Emile-Jacques Ruhlmann, France's leading designer of luxury furniture and interiors, had the task of making sure the interiors lived up to the high ideals of the exposition. Guest countries were accepted only if they agreed to toe the line. Most acquiesced, since they wanted the French market. A journalist assessing the national displays noted that "almost everywhere the will to modernism dominates the craftsman [in] an almost total suppression of ornament." Both Germany and the United States declined to participate.

Aside from the pavilions of the Galleries Lafayette and other department stores, manufacturers created the biggest splash. Car maker Citroën paid for a modernist display of lights on the Eiffel Tower. René Lalique designed a towering glass fountain that lit up at night. The challenge of modernism defeated some designers, who created pavilions of alarming knobbiness but no particular style. One critic compared the Czech building to a grain silo or cold storage warehouse. Others, such as the garden designed by colonial architect Joseph Marrast and realized by the Moser horticultural company, achieved a timeless tranquility. The British magazine *The Studio*, journal of record for the applied arts, couldn't find much to praise in its own national pavilion, but acclaimed French invention. "The new ideas seemed to have come like a flood, carrying all along in its course."

Most agreed that the star of the show was the Hôtel d'un Collectionneur (Private Home of a Collector). Planned by Ruhlmann and housed in a pavilion by architect Pierre Patout, it offered a vision of how a modern collector of discriminating taste and bottomless pockets might furnish his ideal home. It included wall paintings by Jean Dunand and Jean Dupas, sculpture by Antoine Bourdelle and ironwork by Edgar Brandt.

Hôtel d'un Collectionneur

The exposition didn't stop at the Seine. Shops with
innovative window displays lined the Alexandre III
bridge. Couturier Paul Poiret, hopeful of retrieving his
prewar reputation, sold his collection of modern art to
buy three barges. Christening them Amour, Delices and
Orgues—Love, Delights and Organs—names which, he
said, represented "women, always women"—he moored
them alongside the exhibition and turned them into
showrooms for his gowns, as well as textiles, furniture
and accessories from his Atelier Marine workshops.
An esplanade ran along their roofs, descending in wide
steps to the waterline, where visitors arriving by boat
were invited to alight.

Poiret's effort failed. Any improvement in his fortunes
was wiped out by the crash of 1929. Forced to sell
Atelier Marine and its chain of shops, he closed down
permanently—an experience shared by many other
designers. In proving French design and craftsmanship
remained supreme, the Exposition of 1925 achieved its
aims. However, 1929 killed the market for luxury goods.
At the same time, American manufacturers duplicated
French designs using cheap imitations of the silk, wood,
leather and precious metals that enriched the products
of French artistry.

Fashion designer Paul Poiret and his models arrive at the train station, 1925

Paradoxically, however, synthetic fibers, metal plating and plastics made the style of Ruhlmann and other designers universal. René Lalique had already created packaging for François Coty's toiletries, duplicating his molded glass in paper. Edgar Brandt, the master of artisan ironwork, adopted new welding and soldering techniques to create the lifts for Selfridge's department store in London. Lee Lawne's reliefs on the exterior of Rockefeller Center in New York are straight from the Art Déco handbook. Cinemas and theaters all over the world adopted the so-called Streamline Moderne style, a scaled-up adaptation of work by such French architects as André Granet.

Chromed steel, originally a substitute for silver in the detailing of automobiles, emerged as a material in its own right. Bakelite and other resins brought the look of ebony, ivory and tortoiseshell to hair brushes, picture frames, radio sets. With rayon, women could wear dresses as vivid as anything seen in a Paris *defilé*. The modern look invaded typography, signage, publishing, advertising but, above all, movies, which carried Art Déco into the furthest corners of the world. The style reigned until the Second World War introduced a new and, initially, bracing realism.

SEE IT: ART DÉCO STYLE

Considering Art Déco was born in Paris, there are few examples on the scale of New York's Rockefeller Center and its Chrysler Building. Respect for Haussmann's reconstruction of the city in the 1860s discouraged 1920s builders from disturbing his grand design. Art Déco most often turns up in shopfronts, the facades of public buildings, and domestic interiors. An exception is the Palais de Chaillot at Trocadero. Built for yet another Exposition in 1937, the imposing wings of the Palais itself and the cascade of statues and fountains tumbling down to the Seine and the Eiffel Tower beyond create a striking effect.

One of the best examples of domestic Art Déco is rue Mallet-Stevens. This short street contains six houses designed by Robert Mallet-Stevens, one of the most innovative of French architects. They were completed in July 1927 and, despite some later additions, remain impressive. Nearby, on Square du Docteur-Blanche, two houses designed by Le Corbusier and Pierre Jeanneret, Villa Jeanneret and Villa La Roche, have been combined as the Fondation Le Corbusier museum and archives. The Mallet-Stevens buildings are not open to the public, but one can tour Fondation Corbusier (all addresses 16th).

CHAPTER 17

THE MAN WHO SOLD THE EIFFEL TOWER: THE VICTOR LUSTIG AND STAVISKY SCANDALS

"About a year ago," said Henry Miller in 1936, "Ezra Pound wrote me a post-card, asking if I had ever thought about money; what makes it, and how it gets that way. Since then, I have thought about it night and day."

Miller was not alone. Paris attracted men and women eager to get rich quickly. But for each one who made a fortune, a dozen waited to swindle them. In 1911, a lone Italian, Vincenzo Peruggia, stole the Mona Lisa from the Louvre, only to surrender it 28 months later, apparently intact. In 1932, however, an Argentinian con man, Edouardo de Valfierno, claimed he had engineered the

Man looks out on the Eiffel Tower, 1929

theft, and hired an artist named Yves Chaudron to create copies, for which a number of rich but unprincipled collectors paid millions. Even today, a few skeptics continue to claim the painting in the Louvre is one of Chaudron's forgeries.

During the 1920s, sleazy Paris had no more permanent fixture than the shabby guide who flashed an envelope of pornographic postcards which, once you handed over your money, proved to have been switched for views of the Eiffel Tower. It took superior imagination and flair, however, to offer the tower itself for sale.

Gustav Eiffel's creation didn't always enjoy its modern popularity. In the 1920s, plenty of people wanted it gone. They argued it was only ever intended as a temporary structure, no more than an imposing entrance to the *Exposition Universelle* of 1889. Even Eiffel expected it to be demolished, and built it for easy deconstruction. So when, in 1925, a plausible gentleman named Victor Lustig, claiming to be deputy director-general of the Ministry of Posts and Telegraphs, invited five scrap-metal merchants to tender for the concession to demolish it, he found receptive ears.

Austrian-born Lustig had honed his swindling skills on the ocean liners that carried wealthy tourists to France. In his most successful con, he posed as the inventor of a machine that could produce perfect facsimiles of the $100 bill. It took six hours for the note to appear, but the first two or three copies were flawless, right down to the watermark. Clients paid as much as $30,000 to own this miracle of technology. The only $100 bills they ever received, of course, were the few authentic examples Lustig planted inside.

With capital from his money machine, Lustig set himself up in Paris's best hotel, the Crillon. After lavishly

The Palais du Trocadéro from the Eiffel Tower, c. 1920s

entertaining the salvage moguls, he took them by rented limousine to the Eiffel Tower, showed them around as if he owned it, then asked for sealed bids to tear it down. When one dealer, André Poisson, queried the need for secrecy, Lustig, shame-faced, confessed he was actually acting illegally. The government had ordered him to open the project to public tender. If it ever got out that he had gone into business for himself, he would be ruined. It was a brilliant move. Poisson, no stranger to graft, bribed Lustig to accept his bid, and so lost even more than he paid for the illusory scrap-iron rights. Too humiliated to complain to the police when he realized he had been conned, Poisson swallowed his loss. A month later, Lustig was back in Paris, trying the same scam with another group. One of his new marks was smarter, however, and warned the police. Lustig fled to Switzerland, one step ahead of arrest.

Switzerland was also the preferred refuge of France's most dramatic and outrageous swindler of the *années folles*, one whose activities toppled governments, sparked riots, and led to his own violent and ambiguous death.

Jean-Paul Belmondo (2nd from left) in the film, *Stavisky*, 1974

Serge Stavisky was Hollywood's idea of a con man.
In Alain Resnais' 1974 film, *Stavisky*, he was played
by France's most glamorous leading man, Jean-Paul
Belmondo, wearing suits designed by Yves St Laurent.
Stavisky appeared in Paris just as the effects of the 1929
stock market crash began to bite, further devaluing the
already depleted French franc. He socialized with such
music hall stars as Mistinguett, married Arlette Simon,
a former model for Coco Chanel, and lived in a suite at
Claridge's Hotel. He produced stage revues, and bought
two newspapers to make sure his activities received
favorable attention. Surrounded by the wealthy and
the beautiful, and with his bodyguard, Jo-Jo le Terreur,
always at his back, Stavisky became one of the sights of
Paris nightlife.

Once society accepted him at his own valuation, he
revealed a get-rich-quick scheme few could resist. The

French government underwrote a network of *montes de piete* or municipal pawnshops where ordinary French workers, notoriously frugal, could borrow on their few treasures. Through monthly interest on the loans and the sale of unredeemed pledges, the pawnshops returned large profits.

Municipal governments could issue shares or bonds in their pawnshops to raise money for civic improvements. From the cities of Orleans and Bayonne, Stavisky received permission to sell such bonds. As security, he produced an apparently priceless pledge: the emeralds of the King of Ethiopia. Or perhaps it was the diamonds of the Empress of Germany: nobody was really sure. Either way, it hardly mattered. High officials of both local and national governments endorsed Stavisky, big insurance companies guaranteed his operation, and his first investors reaped rich returns.

As people stampeded to buy his bonds, cooler heads warned of the dangers. It emerged that Stavisky was a career crook. Before coming to Paris, he had run illegal gambling clubs on money given to him by wealthy older women, dealt in cocaine from Turkey, and been tried in 1927 for fraud. When his father, a dentist, was unable to repay the money swindled by his son, he killed himself in shame. Stavisky went to jail, but was paroled on suspiciously flimsy health grounds.

Hearing these charges, investors shrugged. As long as the cash flowed, who cared where he got it? Attempts to probe deeper ran up against his well-bribed supporters, who included two chiefs of police, an ambassador, a general, numerous financial journalists, lawyers, magistrates, and the entire staff of France's equivalent of the FBI. Over a six-year period, Stavisky paid out more than $3 million in bribes, listed on his books as "stock dividends." When these people came to trial a year after his death, the weight of paperwork was so huge the investigation was called "the case of 30,000 documents."

Even with so much protection, Stavisky's scheme was doomed. As with subsequent swindlers Charles Ponzi and Bernard Madoff, the need to keep paying out money soon outstripped the amount coming in. Once an expert, examining the Emperor's (or Empress's) jewels, discovered they were glass, his options ran out. Arrested in 1933, Stavisky was released on bail as officials at every level of government tried to cover up their complicity in his frauds. He fled to Switzerland—and was found there in a rented chalet near Chamonix in January 1934, shot in the head. Suicide? If so, why was he lying on the floor while his gun was some distance away on a bed? Stavisky lay bleeding while the police debated this. Finally transported to hospital two hours later, he was found, conveniently, to be dead.

The left-wing government of Camille Chautemps collapsed amid accusations that Stavisky had been murdered to hide the extent of his graft. Jean Chiappe, fascist head of the Paris police, stirred up bloody street riots to protest the alleged cover-up. On February 6, 1934, 15 people died. Two more left-wing prime ministers were forced to resign before a coalition government restored confidence. The new prime minister, Edouard Daladier, fired Chiappe, leading to yet more protests in which his own government also fell.

Arlette Stavisky outlived her husband by more than 50 years. In 1988, returning to Paris after a long absence, she was interviewed by a magazine. "Understand that my husband all by himself was more intelligent than all the journalists of the world put together," she said. It is hard to disagree.

Victor Lustig, 1937 and Serge Stavisky, 1934

SCHEMERS AND SWINDLERS

Serge Stavisky is buried in Pere Lachaise cemetery (20th). The French police are not anxious to remind the public of how its most slippery swindlers operated under their very noses. The official Musée de Police at 4, rue de la Montagne Sainte-Geneviève (5th) mentions neither Lustig nor Stavisky. The Maison de Barreau or headquarters of the French bar, the association of lawyers, is slightly more revealing. Its handsome museum on rue de Harlay (1st) contains documents preserved by lawyers from many famous cases. Among the trials covered are those of Louis XVI and Marie Antoinette, the novelist Emile Zola , whose broadside "*J'Accuse*" defended the wrongly convicted Alfred Dreyfus, writer Robert Brasillach, the Nazi collaborator whose last words before the firing squad were "*Vive la France quand même!*"—*Long live France anyway*!—and Marshal Philippe Petain, who headed the puppet Vichy government during World War II and, though sentenced to death, was never executed. It's fitting that Serge Stavisky is also represented in this ragtag aristocracy with documents relating to his criminal career and the trials of his accomplices. Victor Lustig has no such memorial, though in 1964 Claude Chabrol directed *L'homme qui Vendit la tour Eiffel* in the omnibus film *Les Plus Belles Escroqueries du Monde*, released in English as *The World's Most Beautiful Swindles*.

CHAPTER 18

AS THOUGH IT KNEW: THE UNKNOWN WOMAN OF THE SEINE

Sometime in the 1880s, an image appeared among Paris antiquarians that exercised a puzzling but seductive influence. It was a plaster cast taken from the face of a young woman; probably, to judge from the smoothness of her skin and the softness of her features, no more than a teenager. Her eyes were closed, her hair combed, her lips curved in a smile. She might have been sleeping.

But her admirers soon sensed something sinister about the image, a quality of stillness more often seen in casts taken from the faces and hands of children who died in infancy. They traced the subject of the cast to the Paris morgue, which stood in a seldom-visited park at the edge of the Île de la Cité, at the rear of Notre Dame. Behind a window, 12 tilted black marble slabs held the week's

The Unknown Virgin, Canal de l'Ourcq, Albert Rudomine, 1927

unidentified corpses—*les inconnus*—in the hope that someone would recognize them.

The coroner said that the apparently sleeping girl was, in fact, dead, and, further, a suicide, fished out of the Seine on the Quai du Louvre. As her body was never claimed, she would have been buried with other anonymous corpses in the cemetery that covered the hill of Montparnasse. The admirers nodded soberly. Of course. That explained it! No calm is so complete, so all-embracing as that of death. And no river so accommodating to life and death as the Seine.

English poet Richard LeGallienne was the first to weave a story around the girl now being called *L'Inconnue de la Seine*—The Unknown of the Seine. In *The Worshipper of the Image*, Antony, a young artist browsing in a sculptor's shop in London's market district of Covent Garden becomes "conscious of a presence."

"Someone was smiling near him. He turned, and, almost with a start, found that—as he then thought—it was no living thing, but just a plaster cast among the others, that was thus shining, like a star among the dead. A face not ancient, not modern; but of yesterday, to-day, and for ever."
He buys the cast and takes it home to show his lover Beatrice.
"Drowned in the Seine!" exclaimed Beatrice, growing almost as white as the image.
"Yes! and he said too that the story went that the sculptor who moulded it had fallen so in love with the dead girl, that he had gone mad and drowned himself in the Seine also."
"But the pain, the pity of it."
"That is a part of the beauty, surely. See how happy she looks. Why should we pity one who can smile like that?"

Antony lays the cast on a couch and tucks a black cloak around it. "The image nestled into the cushion as though it had veritably been a living woman weary for sleep." Recognizing she can never compete, Beatrice drowns herself.

The mask held a special appeal for Germans and Austrians. Actress Elizabeth Bergner is said to have modelled her makeup and expression on *L'Inconnue*, and there are echoes of that smiling calm in some performances by Greta Garbo. In his semi-autobiographical *The Notebooks of Malte Laurids Brigge*, the poet Rainer Maria Rilke describes seeing the mask in the shop of a Paris plaster caster—"The face of the young one who drowned, which someone copied in the morgue because it was beautiful, because it was still smiling, because its smile was so deceptive—as though it knew."

In 1926, *Das Ewige Antlitz*, (The Eternal Face) collected images of 123 death masks. The writer could barely contain his admiration of *L'Inconnue*. "To us she is a delicate butterfly," he wrote, "who—winged and lightheartedly—had her tender wings prematurely singed." Albert Camus, who became the poet of Existentialism and wrote one of its most significant works, *L'Etranger*, owned a cast, and was moved by its "smile of a drowned Mona Lisa." In 1933, a publisher asked the novelist Louis-Ferdinand Celine for a photograph of himself. Instead he sent an image of *L'Inconnue*.

In 1934, Reinhold Conrad Muschler's *Die Unbekannte* (One Unknown) became the most popular version of the story. A young orphan, Madeleine Lavin, enjoys a Paris idyll with British diplomat Lord Thomas Vernon Bentick. When he dumps her for his American fiancée and leaves for Egypt, she drowns herself. "Yes Tom" she cries, going

Île de la Cité and the rear of Notre Dame, c. 1920

Flood at Port Saint Nicolas (current Quai du Louvre), 1910

down for the third time. "It's me, I'm coming." The book concludes, "Her face had a transfigured smile when she was found." The first edition sold 175,000 copies. "This fact should cause the admiration and despair of the ever multiplying race of authors," wrote a British reviewer, "for though they may envy, they can hardly hope to emulate its sincere, unaffected and quite nauseating sentimentality."

When the narrator of Anaïs Nin's 1944 story "Houseboat" fires a gun out the window of a houseboat on the Seine, she worries she might injure *L'Inconnue*. To Austrian playwright Ödön von Horváth, she was more robust—a temptress, descendant of Melusine, the mermaid who leaves the water to marry a mortal. His *Inconnue* lures a young man to theft and murder. "I would sing you to sleep," she whispers to her victim, "but the window should be open and when you look out you should have green eyes, big green eyes like a fish." Von Horváth, before leaving Vienna for Paris in 1938, told a friend, "I am not afraid of the Nazis. There are worse things one can be afraid of. For instance, I am afraid of streets. Streets scare me." Rightly so. During a downpour, he took shelter under a tree on the Champs-Élysées, and was killed by a falling branch.

Every year brought a new theory about *L'Inconnue*. Was she really a drowning victim? Was she even French? One researcher identified her as Ewa Lázló, a Hungarian music hall artist murdered by an extortionist, but then admitted he lied. A French investigator, René Vautrain, swore she was a Russian from Saint Petersburg called Valérie. This may have been an invention of Vladimir Nabokov, later the author of *Lolita*, who composed a poem inspired by *Die Unbekannte*. "Amidst pale crowds of drowned young maidens," he wrote, "you're the palest and sweetest of all"—but then suggested she might have killed herself over a lover with a "loud tie and gold-capped tooth."

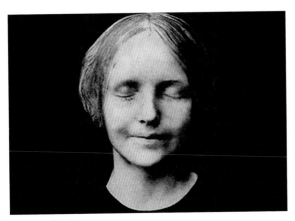

L'Inconnue de la Seine

For an exhibition of death masks at the Musée d'Orsay,
French scholar Hélène Pinet launched the first
thorough investigation of *L'Inconnue*, but found nothing
substantial. The police records showed no evidence of
an unidentified girl of her description. Other sleuths
traced the sighting by Rainer Maria Rilke to Lorenzi's,
a shop on rue Racine, next to the Sorbonne, which sold
plaster models to art students. The mouleurs decisively
dismissed the idea that this was a death mask. In death
the muscles sag, the eyes sink. This woman was alive
when the clay was applied. She might have been a young
model, perhaps even the mold-maker's own daughter.

Could it all be an invention? "The facts were so scarce,"
Hélène Pinet told British journalist Angelique Chrisafis,
"that every writer could project what they wanted on to
that smooth face. Death in water was a very romantic
concept. Death, water and woman was a tantalizing
combination." More than a century after *L'Inconnue*
supposedly threw herself into the fast-flowing waters
of the Seine, the mystery of her placid, smiling face
tantalizes still.

WHERE TO FIND YOUR OWN L'INCONNUE

The workshops of Lorenzi: Moulages d'art are situated at 60, avenue Laplace (Vache Noire) F 94110 Arcueil. They still stock and sell casts of *L'Inconnue*. The Paris mortuary, now on the right bank, near Bastille, was formerly on quai de l'Archevêché (1st), beneath the small park behind the cathedral of Notre Dame. The Mémorial des Martyrs de la Déportation now occupies the site. The Quai du Louvre runs between the rue de l'Amiral Coligny and rue de la Monnaie (1st). It's no longer possible to throw oneself into the Seine at that point (if it ever was) because of the Voie Georges Pompidou running along the river on a lower level. The body of *L'inconnue* may have been fished out there, in which case she probably jumped from one of the nearby bridges, where the river runs fast between stone banks and through the narrow spans of Pont Neuf and the Pont des Arts.

Ödön von Horváth is the central figure of Christopher Hampton's 1982 play *Tales From Hollywood*, which speculates about the playwright's possible career in the movies had he not died in that thunderstorm.

The most unexpected modern reincarnation of *L'Inconnue* is as the face of Resusci Anne, the plastic figure used to demonstrate such lifesaving techniques as mouth-to-mouth resuscitation. More than 300 million people have kissed some version of the model, designed in the 1950s by Norwegian toymaker Asmund Laerdal.

CHAPTER 19

OF THEE I SING: AMERICAN SONGWRITERS IN PARIS

While the name "Paris" has appeared in more songs than any other capital, only a few have conveyed the city's character. "Paris" or "Paree" generally serves as shorthand for sophistication, either in dress, as in Cole Porter's use of "a Paris hat" to signify an expensive gift in "I'm Always True to You Darling In My Fashion," or in behavior, as in the 1918 "How Ya Gonna Keep 'em Down on the Farm After They've Seen Paree?," which enquired of American soldiers returning from France:

How ya gonna keep 'em away from harm, that's a mystery.
Imagine Reuben when he meets his Pa
He'll kiss his cheek and holler "Oo-la-la"

George Gershwin by Edward Steichen, 1927

Gene Kelly and Leslie Caron in *American in Paris*, 1951

Most compositions about Paris have their myths. When "April in Paris" became a hit in the 1932 musical *Walk A Little Faster*, it was reported that composers Vernon Duke and E.Y. Harburg, ignorant of Paris, had asked for a list of events taking place there in April. Informed that, since the weather was so bad, people stayed indoors, they fell back on vague details—"Chestnuts in blossom, holiday tables under the trees." Nevertheless, Duke received a medal from the French government for extending the tourist season by a month. In fact, Duke knew France well. Between 1924 and 1929, he divided his time between New York and Paris. While in France, he composed a ballet, *Zephyr and Flora*, for Serge Diaghilev, and became a lifelong friend of Sergei Prokofiev.

Not all myths are so easily dispelled. Traditionally, George Gershwin used an upright piano in the basement of Harry's Bar on rue Danou to compose his orchestral suite *An American in Paris*. Nobody has yet explained why the wealthy Gershwin needed to work in a bar. When he approached Stravinsky to give him lessons in composition, Stravinsky asked "How much money do you make a year?" On hearing the figure, he said, "Perhaps I should study with you, Mr. Gershwin."

The future creator of *Porgy and Bess* paid his first visit to Paris in 1926 and returned in 1928 at the urging of Maurice Ravel, who thought he might benefit from studying with Nadia Boulanger at the French Music School for Americans in Fontainebleau. After Gershwin played his compositions for 30 minutes, Boulanger told him "I can teach you nothing." Flattered by such a rejection, Gershwin began work on a "rhapsodic ballet" he called *An American in Paris*. It was based on a piece called "Very Parisienne," written during his 1926 visit as a gift to his hosts, music publishers Robert and Mabel Schirmer. "My purpose here," Gershwin wrote of *An American in Paris*, "is to portray the impressions of an American visitor in Paris as he strolls about the city, listens to the various street noises, and absorbs the French atmosphere."

Looking for unique visual signatures, Gershwin noted that, on the exterior of their cars, Paris cabbies carried a trumpet-like horn, which they operated by squeezing a rubber bulb. The sound was distinctive, but varied with manufacturer and age. Gershwin bought used taxi horns from a number of garages and brought them back to the U.S. When the suite premiered at Carnegie Hall on December 13, 1928, the score included a passage for four tuned taxi horns, played by two musicians.

Taxi horns also inspired Richard Rodgers and Lorenz Hart in writing the 1932 screen musical *Love Me Tonight*. Set in Paris, it starred America's favorite Frenchman,

Cole Porter (left), 1913

Maurice Chevalier. He had made his name with the 1929 film *Innocents of Paris*, his first talkie, in which he sang one of his greatest successes, "Louise." Director Rouben Mamoulian conceived an opening number for *Love Me Tonight* in which Paris gradually comes to life in its sounds; women beat carpets, a shoemaker hammers nails, a broom sweeps stairs. Finally, Chevalier wakes and sings "That's the Song of Paree." It includes the typically Hart-esque couplet "We have taxi horns and klaxons/To scare the Anglo-Saxons."

After Gershwin, the American songwriter most associated with Paris was Cole Porter. He arrived in July 1917, supposedly to work for a war relief charity. He later claimed to have taught gunnery to American soldiers at the French Officers School at Fontainebleau, or, alternatively, to have joined the recruiting department of American Aviation Headquarters. Other versions have him serving with the French Foreign Legion in north Africa. In *Night and Day*, a deliciously ridiculous 1946 biopic starring Cary Grant, he's shown leaning against a palm tree, inspired by drums and some softly humming African soldiers to compose "Begin the Beguine" (actually written in 1935 during a Pacific cruise). In its obituary, *The New York Times* wrote, even less probably, that "he had a specially constructed portable piano made for him so that he could carry it on his back and entertain the troops in their bivouacs."

Despite these tales, there are no records of Porter serving in any military capacity at all. "He made up stories about working with the French Foreign Legion and the French army," wrote J.X. Bell in a pungent summary of Porter's Paris years. "This allowed him to live his days and nights as a socialite and still be considered a 'war hero' back home."

He did enroll to study composition with Vincent d'Indy at the Schola Cantorum, a music school set up to teach orchestral writing, as opposed to the opera favored by other conservatoria. Porter purchased a luxurious 18th-century mansion, which he decorated with platinum wallpaper and chairs upholstered in zebra skin. He threw numerous parties, which J.X. Bell describes as "elaborate and fabulous, involving people of wealthy and political classes. His were marked by much gay and bisexual activity, Italian nobility, cross-dressing, international musicians, and a large surplus of recreational drugs."

All the same, Paris exercised a strong and long-lived inspirational influence on Porter. For fellow expatriate Gerald Murphy, who had been with him at Yale, he wrote a symphonic jazz score for his ballet *Within the Quota*. In 1928, his score for the musical *Paris* included the classic comic song "Let's Do It." In 1929, *Fifty Million Frenchmen* included "You Do Something To Me." In 1953, for *Can-Can*, he wrote "I Love Paris." Because of his wife's complaisant attitude to his homosexuality, Porter was also able to enjoy a number of affairs with young men in the European ballet scene, including Diaghilev's last lover, Boris Kochno.

Though some American songs became popular in France, most of the *chansons* heard in the street or in café-concerts were French. With radios and phonographs still rare, songs were made popular by strolling street vocalists who earned their living from tips and from selling sheet music. Without amplification or instrumental accompaniment, they learned to use the resonance of courtyards and narrow streets to boost their voices. Albert Prejean played such a singer in the 1930 film *Sous les Toits de Paris* (*Under the Roofs of Paris*) and made its theme song a national hit. In 1929, 14-year-old Edith Gassion joined her father, a street acrobat, as he travelled the roads of France. In the process, she developed a piercing and poignant singing voice. She became a street singer in Paris's working class districts of Pigalle, Bellville and Menilmontant, and in time, as Edith Piaf, a star.

Cole and Linda Porter, and their home at 5, rue Danou in Paris

SEE IT: COLE PORTER'S HOME, GERSHWIN'S PIANO

Cole Porter's Paris home still stands at 13, rue Monsieur (7th), although the half-timbered house with a large garden is not visible from the street. The Schola Cantorum where he studied is at 269, rue Saint-Jacques (5th).

The piano on which George Gershwin may have composed part of *An American in Paris* has been preserved in the basement of Harry's New York Bar, 5, rue Danou (2nd). *An American in Paris* is mainly remembered for Vincente Minnelli's 1951 film starring Gene Kelly, Leslie Caron, Oscar Levant and French music hall star George Guetary. The score incorporates a number of Gershwin songs, including "I'll Build a Stairway to Paradise," "Our Love Is Here to Stay," "I've Got Rhythm" and "Embraceable You," but the centerpiece is Gene Kelly's 17-minute ballet version of the original orchestral suite. The sequence was designed by Irene Sharaff, who had studied at l'Académie de la Grande Chaumière. Her designs reflect a different artist for each sequence: Raoul Dufy (the Place de la Concorde), Edouard Manet (the flower market), Maurice Utrillo (a Paris street), Henri Rousseau (the fair), Vincent van Gogh (the Place de l'Opera), and Henri de Toulouse-Lautrec (the Moulin Rouge). George Gershwin never lived to see the film. He died in 1937.

CHAPTER 20

BLACK AS THE DEVIL, HOT AS HELL, PURE AS AN ANGEL, SWEET AS LOVE: COFFEE AND THE CAFÉ

In London and Vienna, coffeehouses were commonplace from the mid-1600s, but as the French traditionally socialized at home, the idea took time to catch on in France. Most of Paris's great cafés only date from the mid-19th century.

An exception is the Procope. Traditionally the first café in France, it opened in 1670 opposite the original theater of the *Comedie Française*. Benjamin Franklin,

Au Café, depicting Solita Solano and Djuna Barnes in Paris, Maurice Branger, 1922

ambassador of an emerging United States, patronized it. Danton, Robespierre and other plotters met there to incubate the revolution of 1789. The Procope's back door looked out on the printery of firebrand publisher Jean-Paul Marat, while the guillotine was developed just a few doors away.

In the 1850s, Baron Georges-Eugene Haussmann rebuilt Paris on orders from Emperor Napoleon III. By ruling that no building could be taller than the street on which it stood, Haussmann dictated wide thoroughfares with ample sidewalks. Until then, prosperous Parisians moved round the city by carriage, seldom setting foot in the filthy and dangerous streets. Now they became pedestrians on the new grand boulevards.

Noting the increase in passing trade, a seller of Asian imports at the busy corner of boulevard St. Germain and rue de Rennes put out tables and offered samples of tea and coffee. The brasserie or brewery of Leonard Lipp opposite did the same for his beer. Soon both establishments were crowded with well-dressed men and women, chatting, flirting, writing, sketching but, above all, drinking.

Cafés transformed the way coffee was drunk. To widen its appeal, proprietors created the noisette, a classic express with a dash of milk that gave it the color of a noisette or hazelnut. Americans preferred café allonge, "stretched" with extra hot water into something like brewed coffee. Cafés also introduced tea, wine, spirits, even, grudgingly, coffee with milk.

When coffee first arrived from Turkey, only men drank it, the stronger the better. Prince Talleyrand, adviser to Napoleon I, famously took his "as black as the devil, hot as hell, pure as an angel, sweet as love." Women found it too bitter, until they learned an Austrian custom of adding honey and cream. Known as café au lait but more correctly café crème, sweetened coffee with milk or cream became popular as a morning drink, enjoyed at home, mostly by women. The male society of the cafés scorned it. Even today, no Parisian drinks a crème after midday. To do so would be like ordering cornflakes for lunch. However, in mixing sweet and bitter, dark and light, women sensed an almost mystical and erotic symbolism. "He was my cream, I was his coffee," said African-American entertainer Joséphine Baker of a white lover, "and when you poured us together, it was something."

For people living in unheated rooms with inadequate sanitation, the café became a literal home-from-home. They washed up in its restroom, ate a breakfast of coffee and rolls at the zinc, then took a table to write, sketch, scheme or just loaf. Periodically they would order another coffee, an absinthe or a cognac with water, known as a *fine a l'eau*. Waiters served a different saucer with each type of drink. As long as the saucers mounted steadily and you paid before leaving, a person could loiter all day. If a regular client nodded off, waiters had orders not to disturb him.

During the 1920s, national, political or artistic groups made certain cafés their own. The Surrealists met every evening at a café on Place Blanche in Montmartre. The Rotonde was the recognized headquarters of the Spanish community. Each afternoon, a *peña* or salon convened there, chaired by the senior resident intellectual. Musicians, choral singers, artist's models, small-time actors and typesetters all had their preferred cafés where employers could come in search of a last-minute replacement. At the musicians' café, to simplify choice, each person carried a symbol of his instrument— violin bow, trumpet mouthpiece, or a clarinet or saxophone reed in his hatband.

Menu for La Rotonde, Albert Fernand Renault, c. 1930

The form of the modern French café evolved in response to economics. Each has a bar where drinks are prepared, a room with tables, chairs and banquettes, and a *terrasse* outside. Prices are lowest if one stands at the bar, known, from the metal that faced it, as the zinc. You pay more if you occupy a table (to cover the waiter's wages) and more again for a place on the *terrasse*, since sidewalk space must be rented from the city.

Having begun as shops, cafés originally served no food beyond croissants or a hard-boiled egg. Clients left the café to eat lunch and dinner in a restaurant, but returned for a *digestif* and to continue with the day's work or socializing. Out of consideration for the staff, most were forbidden to stay open all night. An exception was made for cafés patronized by professionals forced to work unsocial hours, such as journalists and prostitutes.

World War I transformed the café yet again. In Montparnasse, such well-established cafés as the Dôme, the Rotonde, the Select and the Closerie des Lilas expanded to accommodate tourists fleeing Prohibition America in search of bohemia and booze. Though regular clients resented this foreign invasion, café owners welcomed them. Tourists drank in the late afternoon and early evening, when locals were still at work, so this influx doubled their clientele. *Terrasses* expanded, cane chairs and tables spilling onto the sidewalks. Canadian Morley Callaghan wrote of the Dôme in 1929, "not long ago it had merely been a zinc bar with a small terrace. Now it was like the crowded bleachers of an old ballpark, the chairs and tables set in low rows extending as far as the next café, the Coupole." As Americans demanded the cocktails the French never drank, larger cafés added *bars Americaines.* Others became *cafés concerts*, offering singers and music. Performers played to people seated at tables—the origin of modern cabaret.

In 1927, two restaurateurs from the Auvergne, Ernest Fraux and René Lafon, opened La Coupole. With a café running along boulevard de Montparnasse, a large restaurant behind it, the *bar americain* along one wall and a dancehall in the basement, it offered everything the tourist, or *café habitué,* could desire, under the single all-embracing cupola that gave the place its name. Literary and artistic Paris flocked to La Coupole. It

Café du Dôme, 1936

became the agreed meeting place of the artists known as
les Montparnos, including André Derain, Fernand Leger,
Chaim Soutime, Moise Kisling, and the photographers
Man Ray and Brassai.

Model Alice Prin, aka Kiki of Montparnasse, danced on
its tables. and Joséphine Baker cuddled up to Georges
Simenon, creator of the detective Maigret. André
Breton, the "pope of Surrealism," indulged in a slapping
match with painter Giorgio de Chirico and thereafter
forbade his followers from patronizing the Coupole. His
deputy Louis Aragon disobeyed, and met his lifetime
companion, Elsa Triolet, there. At the zinc, Aragon also
counseled two young Spanish artists, Luis Buñuel and
Salvador Dalí, and introduced them to Man Ray. And
when the music hall star Mistinguett made her entrance
surrounded by her boys, including lover Maurice
Chevalier, les Montparnos stood to applaud her. As with
many other staid features of French culture, *les années
folles* lit up the institution of the café, and exported it to
every corner of the world. It's with us still.

SEE IT: THE LEGENDARY CAFÉS OF PARIS

When the pioneering storeowner on boulevard St. Germain abandoned chinoserie for coffee, he retained two statues of Chinese merchants or *megots* from his stock. Still in place, they inspired his café's name: Aux Deux Magots (6th). Brasserie Lipp continues to function also, along with the nearby Café Flore. In Montparnasse, the Dôme, Rotonde, Select and Coupole (all 14th) are now café restaurants, where anyone wanting a simple express will be exiled to a corner in favor of clients wanting lunch or dinner. The *terrasse* at the Closerie des Lilas is now part of its expensive restaurant but in the bar the tables bear brass plates with the names (mostly misspelled) of the literary figures who once drank there.

The zinc may now be stainless steel or aluminum, but coffee drunk at the bar remains the cheapest. Buying an express also authorizes you to browse one of the free newspapers and use the café's toilette. And if it's your birthday and you call a day ahead, La Coupole will still dim the lights as waiters carry a cake with a lighted candle to your table and harmonize on "Joyeuse Anniversaire."

La Coupole on boulevard Montparnasse

CHAPTER 21

LITTLE GENTLEMEN: GAY AND LESBIAN PARIS

In the Victorian era, homosexuality, because of its illegality, had become what Oscar Wilde called "the love that dare not speak its name." Gay men in Britain were reduced to such euphemisms as "I have an unusual temperament." Others, with a wink, asked new acquaintances if they were "musical," or "so," i.e., "that way."

That France had decriminalized homosexuality in 1791 helped make Paris, along with Berlin, the most gay of Europe's capitals. Those not lucky enough to live there would experience the city vicariously through the erotic books and magazines published there, others through the reminiscences of more audacious friends. English novelist Christopher Isherwood was able to live in Berlin courtesy of an elderly relative who paid him an allowance, providing he described his sexual adventures in detail when he returned to Britain.

Au Monocle, Brassaï,1932

"I invented lesbianism," declared Parisian hostess Natalie Clifford Barney. When friends demurred, she said defiantly, "Well, nobody talked about it before I did." This wasn't entirely untrue. Being from a wealthy Ohio family and having sat on Oscar Wilde's knee as a girl, she was well placed to explore her sexuality. At 23, she moved to Paris and, dressed as a page boy, presented herself in the dressing room of the bisexual music-hall star and courtesan Liane de Pougy, announcing she was a "page of love." De Pougy documented their subsequent affair in her best-selling 1901 novel *Idylle Saphique* (*Sapphic Idyll*).

Idylle Saphique established Barney as the doyenne of Paris's lesbian community. In the grounds of her house on rue Jacob, she built a Greek temple dedicated to "friendship." At performances in the garden, friends danced in Greek robes while others recited poems by Sappho. Her weekly salon attracted literary figures, gay and otherwise, from around the world. She inspired a character in Radclyffe Hall's pioneering lesbian novel *The Well of Loneliness*, and was parodied by Djuna Barnes in her 1928 mock-Elizabethan satire *The Ladies Almanack* as Dame Evangeline Musset, "who was so much in Demand, and so wide famed for her Genius at bringing up by Hand, and so noted and esteemed for her Slips of the Tongue that it finally brought her into the Hall of Fame."

Such self-publicists as Barney gave hope to homosexuals forced to hide their sexuality. Those who moved to Paris found a thriving gay culture, including many literary and artistic women who, while more discreet than Barney, lived openly as lesbians or, like the novelist Colette, made no secret of their bisexuality. They included Gertrude Stein and Alice B. Toklas, American writer Djuna Barnes, Janet Flanner, who as "Genet," was *The New Yorker's* Paris correspondent,

Sylvia Beach, proprietor of Shakespeare and Company, and fellow bookseller Adrienne Monnier, such painters as Romaine Brooks and the Australian Agnes Goodsir, Oscar Wilde's niece Dolly, and many others less famous.

Although Oscar Wilde fled to Paris and died there, the city held less attraction for male gays, who preferred Germany, since, as Christopher Isherwood memorably explained, "Berlin meant boys." All the same, Paris had numerous gay celebrities, in particular the poet and artist Jean Cocteau and novelists Marcel Proust and André Gide. "*Les petits monsieurs*"—(the little gentlemen)—were welcomed in fashionable society for their wit and cultivation. When music hall star Yvette Guilbert suggested in 1930 that hosts of dinner parties should revive the custom of having a singer perform "between the pear and the cheese," one magazine joked that the young girls whose simple recitations ended family dinners in the 19th century had been replaced by flamboyant gays who, with a little encouragement, would sing songs as outrageous as those of the innocents had been demure.

As part of the predominantly gay circle around Serge Diaghilev and the Ballets Russes, Cocteau was further out of the closet than many, though he still disguised his taste for sailors and working-class men. His memoir *Le Livre Blanc* (*The White Book*), appeared only anonymously in 1927. He later agreed he had written it, but declined to take credit for the explicit drawings of well-hung farm boys and sailors. His more romantic liaisons, in particular with novelist Raymond Radiguet and actor Jean Marais, were common knowledge. In 1930, he premiered his play *The Human Voice*, in which a woman, alone on stage, carries on a long telephone conversation with an unseen lover. At the first night, when the telephone rang, jokers in the audience shouted "It's Jean Desbordes!"—Cocteau's current companion.

Barbette, Man Ray, 1926

Once tourists began to flood into Paris, its gay subculture became yet another aspect of the city's "naughtiness." There is a puritanical mixture of lubriciousness and distaste in a 1927 guide book's descriptions of such establishments as La Petite Chaumiere. "This is a place where men dress as women: men of a certain degenerate tendency who infest every large city. If, however you do want to see these Freaks cavort around and swish their skirts and sing in Falsetto and shout 'whoops, my dear' this is the place to see them."

The guide goes on to mention "Chez Roland, Chez Ma Belle Soeur, La Triboulette and the Angel Bar, Champs Elysees Bar and the Liberty Bar. The Fairy-Nice Boys are thick in these places." As it implies, dressing *en travesti* was widely practiced in Paris. Under the stage name Barbette, cross-dressing Texas-born acrobat Vander Clyde became a star of the French music hall. Although a British entrepreneur cancelled his contract when he found him having sex with another man backstage, Clyde was taken up enthusiastically by the Paris demi-monde. He was photographed by Man Ray and had a brief affair with Cocteau, who described him as "no mere acrobat in women's clothes, nor just a graceful daredevil, but one of the most beautiful things in the theatre. Stravinsky, Auric, poets, painters, and I myself have seen no comparable display of artistry on the stage since Nijinsky."

Numerous clubs and dance halls, including one of the largest, Magic City, welcomed or at least tolerated same-sex dancing and drag. The most fashionable lesbian club was Le Monocle, which required that members wear male dress clothing. In 1932, photographer Brassai was impressed by the club's seriousness. "A tornado of virility had gusted through the place and blown away all the tricks of feminine coquetry, changing women

Magic City ballroom

into boys, gangsters, policemen. Obsessed by their unattainable goal to be men, they wore the most somber uniforms; black tuxedos, as though in mourning for their ideal masculinity."

Periodically the Anglo-Saxon world made a stand against the toleration in France of acts which, in Britain and the United States, were a crime. In his 1926 play *La Prisonnière*, a hit on the Paris stage, Edouard Bourdet's heroine refuses to leave Paris with her diplomat father because she is in love with an older married woman. Instead she persuades a friend to marry her as a way of remaining in Paris. After a year of this "white marriage," however, she deserts him for her lesbian lover. As *The Captive*, the play ran 17 weeks on Broadway but suffered the same fate as the English translation of Victor Margueritte's novel *La Garçonne*. In both cases, moralists forced the police to intervene. The cast of *The Captive* were charged with indecency, and the management agreed to close the play.

Had the forces of law and order but known, at least one marriage of convenience engineered by a determined lesbian already existed in Paris. In 1921, homosexual writer and editor Robert McAlmon married Annie Winifred Ellerman, otherwise known as Bryher, the lesbian heiress to a shipping fortune. In this way Ellerman could live in Paris with her lover, the poet Hilda Doolittle, without scandalizing her father. McAlmon used her money to start Contact Press, which published a number of important books, including Gertrude Stein's *The Making of Americans* and Ernest Hemingway's *Three Stories and Ten Poems*. Nobody was horrified, although McAlmon had to endure being known as "Robert McAlimony."

THE LEGENDARY HAUNTS OF THE ANNÉES FOLLES

Of the famous gay venues of the *années folles*, none survive. The Magic City *bal musette* was at 188, rue de l'Université (7th). Others clustered around the Bastille, mostly on rue de Lappe (11th), a notorious hangout for petty gangsters and *apaches*. From 1932 to 1940, lesbian club Le Monocle operated in the basement at 14 boulevard Edgar Quinet (14th). Gay cafés in Montmartre included La Folie, rue Victor Masse (9th), Chez Ma Cousine, rue Lepic, La Petite Chaumiere, 2, rue Berthe, Chez Ma Belle Soeur, 47, rue Cauliancourt, and Tonton, rue Norvins (all 18th), Chez Roland, 15, rue Aux Ours, and Chez Julie, rue Saint Martin (both 3rd), and La Triboulette, 243, rue Saint Jacques (5th). Such names as "Chez Ma Cousine" or "Chez Ma Belle Soeur" (at my cousin's or my sister-in-law's place) allowed visitors to be discreet about where they spent their evenings.

Famous cross-dresser/performer Vander Clyde retired in the late 1930s because of ill-health. He returned to the U.S. and became a consultant and coach for the circus and movies. His performances inspired that of Julie Andrews in the film *Victor Victoria*. He also advised Jack Lemmon and Tony Curtis on impersonating women in *Some Like It Hot*. He committed suicide in 1973.

CHAPTER 22

THE RAZOR AND THE EYE: LUIS BUÑUEL, SALVADOR DALÍ, AND SURREALISM

Few images in cinema are as memorable as the first shots of the 1929 *Un Chien Andalou* (*An Andalusian Dog*) by Salvador Dalí and Luis Buñuel. A man in shirt-sleeves steps onto a balcony at night, cigarette smoldering between his lips, straight razor in hand. As sharp-edged clouds slide across the moon, he turns to a seated girl and draws the razor across her eye.

More than 80 years later, this sequence still has power to shock. Knowing the eye isn't human but belongs to a dead calf doesn't help. Nor does the overt symbolism—"Open your eyes!" As vitreous humor oozes around the

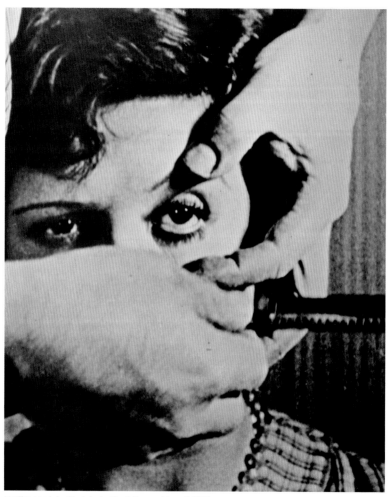

Un Chien Andalou (Andalusian Dog), Simone Mareuil, 1929

steel, we shudder.

The man with the razor is Luis Buñuel. Then 28, he had come to Paris from rural eastern Spain. His wealthy parents thought he was awaiting a diplomatic job; actually he hoped to make movies. He told friends in Madrid he was friendly with Paris's artistic elite, including its most glamorous intellectuals, the Surrealists. In fact, all he had done in four years was find a French girlfriend and become a familiar figure around the bars of Montparnasse. His cinema career consisted of a few lowly jobs as production assistant, and reviewing films for Spanish magazines. As for the elusive, insular Surrealists, they kept to Montmartre and he hadn't met even one of them.

Buñuel was ready to quit and open a bar, but his mother refused to finance him; gentlemen did not sell booze. She did, however, give him the same sum that each of his sisters received as a dowry when they married. It wasn't sufficient to produce a feature film, but it might finance a short.

To help on the film, Buñuel approached a friend from his college days in Madrid. Salvador Dalí, four years younger, was also from a wealthy provincial family, but any similarities ended there. Dalí was slim and intense where Buñuel was muscular and athletic, mercurial where Buñuel was impassive, spontaneous where Buñuel was practical, and sexually ambivalent where Buñuel was an enthusiastic (if repressed) heterosexual. Of Dalí's infantile and often bizarre sexual tastes, Buñuel said later, he "seduced many ladies, particularly American ladies, but these seductions usually consisted of stripping them naked in his apartment, frying a couple of eggs, putting them on the woman's shoulders and, without a word, showing them the door."

Luis Buñuel

The most obvious disparity was in talent. At college, where Buñuel and Dalí had made a trio with a young gay poet from Andalusia, Federico Garcia Lorca, Buñuel was by far the least accomplished. Dalí and Lorca, both prodigies, became even closer—until Lorca tried to introduce his friend to sodomy. "I was extremely annoyed," Dalí said, "because I wasn't homosexual, and I wasn't interested in giving in. Besides, it hurts."

Hoping to pick Dalí's brains, Buñuel showed him a script he had created with popular author Gomez de la Serna. Dalí found it "extremely mediocre," while claiming, with typical self-importance, that he had "just written a very short scenario which had the touch of genius." Dalí wanted to explore Surrealism, but still wasn't sure he understood its more obscure rules. "The point of Surrealism," he said, "was to transcribe thought without any rational, aesthetic or moral checks." And where better to show pure thought and fantasy than in the medium closest to the unconscious, cinema?

The Paris Surrealists, 1933: Tristan Tzara, Paul Éluard, André Breton, Hans Arp, Salvador Dalí, Yves Tanguy, Max Ernst, René Crevel and Man Ray. Photo by Anna Riwkin-Brick

Luis and Salvador retreated to Cadaques, a fishing village near Buñuel's family home. Once Dalí admitted he had no scenario, just some vague ideas, they started to invent one. "Our only rule was simple," said Buñuel. "No idea or image that might lend itself to a rational explanation of any kind would be accepted. We had to open all doors to the irrational and keep only those images that, without trying to explain why, surprised us."

They used this same spontaneous method to choose a title—the nonsensical *Dangereux de se Pencher en Dedans* (*Dangerous to Lean Outside*), a notice posted in every railway carriage. During shooting, however, and with Lorca in mind, Buñuel substituted *Un Chien Andalou*. Lorca recognized the insult. "Buñuel has made a little film," he said. "It's called *Un Chien Andalou*—and I'm the dog!"

There's no Lorca in the film, and no dog. Incidents flow with the logic of dream—or nightmare. A man in frilly clothing and a box around his neck cycles down a Paris avenue. When he falls off, a girl runs out to help him. Later, a severed hand lies in the street. An androgyne with a mannish haircut pokes it with a stick and is run down by a car. The man bursts into an apartment, his hand crawling with ants. The girl appears, triggering images of a sea urchin in her hairy armpit. He caresses her in imagination, but when he tries to cross the room to be with her, he is suddenly dragging ropes to which are attached priests and grand pianos crammed with the carcasses of dead donkeys. To possess the woman, he merely has to drop the ropes, but is unable to do so . . . .

Buñuel directed the film alone. Dalí only appeared for the last two days of the 15-day shoot, in time to play one of the priests. But there was no doubting the subtext of the film; the attack on the repressive attitude of the church towards sex, and the burdens it imposed on intellectual and sensual freedom; burdens as ridiculous as pianos loaded down with dead donkeys.

Showing the practicality that would carry him through a long career, Buñuel called in every favor, cut every corner. His girlfriend Jeanne sewed the costumes and kept the books. With no money for laboratory work, he created dissolves and fades by winding back the film inside the camera. The main actor, Pierre Batcheff, was a friend from a film on which he had worked as assistant. So was the cameraman. Fano Messan, a young sculptor who bobbed her hair in *garçonne* style, played the girl in the street.

However, once he screened the film, Buñuel despaired. "I was absolutely sure it was going to be a failure," he said. The censors were certain to ban it. As for the Surrealists, nobody had yet made a Surrealist film. Did *Un Chien Andalou* deserve the title? The "pope" of the movement, André Breton, jealously protected the name, organizing raids on those who misused it. When dancer Valeska Gert offered a program of what she called *Ballets Surrealistes*, their whistles and insults drove her from the stage.

The filmmakers were saved by Denise Batcheff, wife of the movie's main actor. She knew Breton's deputy Louis Aragon, and arranged for him to see *Un Chien Andalou*. To him, it seemed Surrealist, but only Breton could say for sure.

To force the issue, he offered to present *Un Chien Andalou* at the screening of a new short film by Man Ray, *Les Mystères du Château de Dé* (*The Mysteries of the Chateau of Dice*), commissioned by the Count and Countess de Noailles. Breton didn't show up, but the celebrity audience was ecstatic. Overnight, Buñuel and Dalí were stars. Producer Pierre Braunberger bought the screening rights. Jean-Georges Auriol published the script in *La Revue du Cinema*. The Noailles invited Dalí and Buñuel to their mansion to commission another.

Breton waited until the cinema release to see the film *Un Chien Andalou*, but he already knew he would approve it. His movement, mostly made up of writers, had been losing members. He needed recruits from new areas, and the visual arts were the most promising. In November, he invited Dalí and Buñuel to attend a Surrealist séance in Montmartre, a formal sign of acceptance.

His decision would shatter Surrealism. Painting and film, more accessible than poetry and prose, increasingly set the agenda. Dalí moved to the United States, unleashed his talent for self-advertisement, and began announcing "I am Surrealism." Furious, Breton rearranged the letters of his name to create a new one—Avida Dollars, i.e., hungry for money. Once Breton and poet Paul Éluard were invited to a Surrealist conference in the Canary Islands in 1935, but only on condition they brought with them a copy of *Un Chien Andalou*, Breton knew the movement he launched was no longer under his control.

RAISE A GLASS TO SURREALISM

Buñuel's original screenplay, with the first title crossed out and *"Un Chien Andalou"* written in, is held by the *Cinematheque Française*. He shot the film in the Billancourt studios at Boulogne, which no longer exist. The Hôtel des Terrasses, where he lived at the time, has also been demolished. When he returned to Paris in the 1960s, he took a room at the Hôtel Aiglon, on the corner of boulevard Auguste Blanqui and boulevard Raspail (14th). Though he chose the hotel for its view of Montparnasse Cemetery, he particularly requested there be no funeral on his own death, and that his grave go unmarked.

The traditional method of saluting Buñuel's memory is to drink one or more Buñuelonis–his variation on the Negroni. The recipe is as follows: one measure red vermouth, one measure white vermouth, three-quarter measure gin. Twist of orange and lemon peel. To be drunk in a bar in mid-afternoon. Buñuel defined the perfect bar as "an exercise in solitude. It must be quiet, dark, very comfortable–no music of any kind, no more than a dozen tables, and a client that doesn't like to talk."

CHAPTER 23

THE HEAVYWEIGHT CHAMPION OF MONTPARNASSE: HEMINGWAY'S KNOCKOUT

Few sportsmen figure among Nobel laureates, and even fewer in the literature category. An exception was Ernest Hemingway, who, with mixed success, tried big game hunting, sport fishing, skiing, bullfighting and, most tenaciously, boxing.

The painter and writer Percy Wyndham Lewis, calling on his friend poet Ezra Pound in the late 1920s, wrote "A splendidly built young man, strip to the waist, and with a torso of dazzling white, was standing not far from me. He was tall, handsome and serene, and was repelling with his boxing gloves—I thought without undue

Ernest Hemingway and Robert McAlmon in Spain, c. 1923

exertion—a hectic assault of Ezra's. After a final swing at the dazzling solar plexus (parried effortlessly by the trousered statue) Pound fell back upon the settee. The young man was Hemingway."

Hemingway could easily defend himself against a vigorous amateur like Pound but he met his match in a bloody encounter in 1929, for which, improbably, Scott Fitzgerald kept time. His opponent was Morley Callaghan, a Canadian writer with whom he had worked on the *Kansas City Star*. An admirer, Callaghan arrived in Paris and immediately looked up his former colleague. They were soon drinking together in such Montparnasse haunts as the Dingo Bar, where Hemingway and Fitzgerald first met.

Callaghan and Hemingway sparred and rough-housed around the large apartment on rue Ferou, which Ernest occupied with his second wife, Pauline Pfeiffer. Even in play, he didn't pull punches. Callaghan recalled, "My wife remembers how, when I came home, she would complain that my shoulders were black and blue. Laughing, I would explain that she should feel thankful; the shoulder welts and bruises meant Ernest had always missed my jaw or nose or mouth."

Increasingly sensing Callaghan as a rival, Hemingway challenged him to a real fight. Even though Callaghan was a foot shorter and 25 pounds overweight, he agreed. "He had given time and imagination to boxing," he said of Hemingway. "I had actually worked out a lot with good fast college boxers." Hemingway relied on his height and weight. But Callaghan, a skillful and seasoned boxer, knew that fast footwork and accurate punching will wear down a larger opponent.

Though, later, Hemingway spoke of a single clash with Callaghan, there were several, spread over the winter of 1929. In earlier bouts, Callaghan proved his skill, ducking Hemingway's punches while landing most of his own. One blow split Hemingway's lip. They boxed on for a few seconds. Then Ernest lowered his gloves and spat a mouthful of blood into Callaghan's face. "That's what the bullfighters do when they are wounded," he said conversationally. "It's a way of showing contempt." Wiping away the blood, an astonished Callaghan wondered "out of what strange nocturnal depths of his mind had come the barbarous gesture."

Some weeks later, Hemingway proposed a rematch. Expecting they would once again spar informally for half an hour, Callaghan was surprised when his friend arrived at his apartment with Scott Fitzgerald, who had agreed, explained Hemingway, to act as timekeeper.

That Hemingway would invite the much less sporty Fitzgerald to officiate at a boxing match was almost as unlikely as him accepting, since the only exercise taken by the *Great Gatsby* author was to lift a glass. His acquiescence reflected a complicated relationship with Hemingway. As Norman Mailer wrote, "Fitzgerald was one of those men who do not give up early on the search to acquire more manhood for themselves. His method was to admire men who were strong." Fitzgerald may have believed that, if he could not face his hero in combat, he could at least take part as a helper.

For his part, Hemingway probably wished the reverse: to destroy the intimacy they had built up. He had already told Callaghan he was avoiding Fitzgerald because he was a drunk and a nuisance. Other expatriates hinted at a more devious motive. Robert McAlmon, homosexual proprietor of the Contact Press, which published Hemingway's first book, circulated a rumor, entirely unsubstantiated, that Hemingway and Fitzgerald were secret lovers. The suggestion would have repelled the

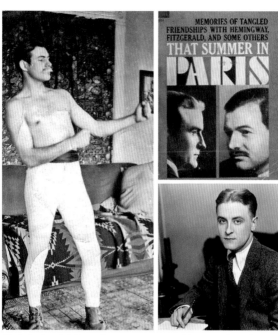

Clockwise from left: Ernest Hemingway wearing a fake mustache and pretending to box, c. 1920; *That Summer in Paris*, Morley Callaghan, 1963; F. Scott Fitzgerald, 1921

ultra-masculine Hemingway, who may have seen the fight as a way to reaffirm his macho reputation.

A taxi took the three men to the American Club, which used the premises of the American Chamber of Commerce. There was no gym; just a basement with a ring marked out on the cement floor. Demonstrating that he took the bout seriously, Hemingway had brought heavy professional boxing gloves. Before he and Callaghan put them on, Hemingway coached Fitzgerald on the duties of the timekeeper—mainly to call "Time" at the end of each three-minute round.

Callaghan sensed that Hemingway regarded this bout as in some way a title fight to humiliate both Fitzgerald and Callaghan, and establish his supremacy both as writer and man of action. If so, he was disappointed. Within a minute of the first round, Callaghan scored solid blows on his opponent's face. When Fitzgerald called "Time" to end the first round, Hemingway was flushed and his lip swollen.

In the second round, Callaghan bored in, punching hard. Hemingway's lip began to bleed again. Fearing that he would again spit blood in his face, Callaghan swung hard and knocked him to the floor.
"Oh my God," Fitzgerald said as Hemingway lay dazed. "I let the round go four minutes."
Climbing to his feet, Hemingway said furiously, "If you want to see me getting the shit knocked out of me, just say so. Only don't say you made a mistake." He stormed away to take a shower.

"I could only stare blankly at Scott," said Callaghan, "who, as his eyes met mine, looked sick. Lashing out with those bitter, angry words, Ernest had practically shouted that he was aware Scott had some deep hidden animosity toward him."

To Callaghan, the issue looked more complicated. "Is the animosity in Scott," he wondered, "or is it really in Ernest?" Perhaps, in Hemingway's mind, the contender for the literary championship of Montparnasse was not Callaghan but Fitzgerald.

Some months later, Callaghan returned to Canada. The story might have ended there, as just another Montparnasse anecdote, had a journalist not written a garbled version of the bout for the *New York Herald Tribune*. It suggested that Hemingway had disparaged Callaghan's work, and that Callaghan challenged him to a match and knocked him out.

Stung, but too proud to respond in person, Hemingway bullied Fitzgerald into protesting on his behalf. Fitzgerald cabled Callaghan "HAVE SEEN STORY IN HERALD TRIBUNE. ERNEST AND I AWAIT YOUR CORRECTION." Callaghan denied leaking the story. He did, however, write to the *Herald Tribune*, setting the reporter straight.

Hemingway remained unsatisfied. "To be knocked down by a smaller man," wrote Norman Mailer, "could only imprison him further into the dread he was forever trying to avoid." In a letter to Callaghan, Hemingway admitted egging Fitzgerald into demanding a retraction, but at the same time tried to keep the feud going. "If you wish to transfer to me the epithets you applied to Scott," he wrote stiffly, "I will be in the States in a few months and am at your disposal." Even more surprising, he suggested a rematch. It had been an error to use heavy professional gloves, he said. "I honestly believe that with small gloves I could knock you out inside of about five two-minute rounds."

Callaghan was too respectful of his old friend to take the bait. Thereafter their relationship deteriorated. For the rest of his life, Hemingway systematically rewrote his account of the fight. In a letter to his editor Maxwell Perkins, he claimed he had been drunk. "I had a date to box with [Callaghan] at 5 p.m.—lunched with Scott and John Bishop at Pruniers—ate Homard thermidor—all sorts of stuff—drank several bottles of white burgundy. Knew I would be asleep by five ... I couldn't see him hardly—had a couple of whiskeys en route ... "

In the same letter, Hemingway suggested Fitzgerald let the crucial round go not for four minutes but eight. By 1951, describing the incident to Fitzgerald's biographer Arthur Mizener, the figure had risen to 13. He would rewrite his entire experience of Paris in the same way.

Finally, the posthumous *A Moveable Feast*, heavily
fictionalized, disparaged Fitzgerald as "poor Scott,"
a pathetic drunk in thrall to a mad, malicious Zelda.
The memoir left Hemingway the last man standing,
undisputed heavyweight champion of Montparnasse.

HEMINGWAY'S HUNTERS, BOXERS, AND BULLFIGHTERS

All his life, Hemingway required male friends to prove their
manhood by taking a physical risk. During a visit to Spain, he
shoved Donald Ogden Stewart, his model for Bill Gorton in *The
Sun Also Rises*, into a ring with a young bull. His fiction consistently
showed bullfighters, hunters and game fishermen as figures of
sexual potency. In "The Short Happy Life of Francis Macomber," an
amateur hunter in Africa shows cowardice when charged by a lion.
Contemptuous, his wife sleeps with the professional hunter leading
the safari. When the husband redeems himself by facing down a
buffalo, she shoots him—whether by accident or design isn't clear.

About boxing, Hemingway was boastful to a degree that shook his
compatriots. He startled novelist Josephine Herbst by saying "My
writing is nothing. My boxing is everything." Before challenging
Morley Callaghan, he had already boxed with Ezra Pound and Harold
Loeb, who inspired the character of Robert Cohn in *The Sun Also
Rises*—an incident used in the novel. Boxing also appears in such
short stories as "Fifty Grand" and "The Battler." In later years, he built
a ring at his Key West house. When locals protested his success in
game fishing tournaments, he invited them to settle matters in the
ring, and supposedly knocked down all comers.

CHAPTER 24

A HALF-CRAZED CAD: THE WILD RIDE OF HARRY AND CARESSE CROSBY

Few expatriates in 1920s Paris cut such a dash as Harry Sturgis Crosby. Tall and startlingly handsome but with a nervous, self-destructive nature, he alarmed and charmed equally. Sylvia Beach at Shakespeare and Company found him delightful. "He used to dart in and out of my bookshop, dive into the bookshelves like a hummingbird extracting honey from a blossom, or hover a minute around my table to tell me that it was he who had told his wife one day that her name was Caresse, and had gone hand in hand with her to the *mairie* to have it legalized." Others were not so impressed. Edith Wharton, who met him through Walter van Rensselaer Berry, the cultivated bibliophile and friend of Marcel Proust and Henry James, sniffed "Walter's young cousin turns out to be a sort of half-crazed cad."

Harry and Caresse Crosby at the Four Arts Ball, Paris, 1922

Born in the conservative Back Bay district of Boston, Crosby was the nephew of financier J. Pierpont Morgan. When war broke out in 1914, he left his job at the Morgan bank to drive an ambulance in France. In November 1917, a shell vaporized his vehicle. Unlike Ernest Hemingway, who survived a similar attack at the cost of shrapnel in his legs, Crosby's only wounds were psychological. Dizzy with the images of death and resurrection that would haunt his short life, he wrote deliriously of "the hills of Verdun, and the red sun setting back of the hills and the charred skeletons of trees and the river Meuse and the black shells spouting up in columns along the road to Bras and the thunder of the barrage and the wounded and the ride through red explosions and the violent metamorphose from boy into man."

Repatriated back to Boston, he started an affair with a woman as much a renegade as himself. Polly Peabody had already scandalized her family by designing and patenting a backless brassiere, and horrified her snobbish in-laws by arriving for her wedding with bobbed hair and pink fingernails, wearing fishnet stockings and a red velvet coat trimmed with monkey fur. When her husband proved to be an alcoholic with, moreover, a passion for house fires, to the extent of installing an alarm in their home connected direct to the firehouse, she accrued further disapproval by divorcing him, taking their two children.

Already an outcast, she didn't hesitate when Harry Crosby proposed to her by telegram from France. To signify her break with Boston, Polly abandoned her name in favour of Harry's more sensual suggestion, Caresse. They took an apartment on rue de Lille, and later bought and restored a mill on the estate of the Duc de la Rochefoucauld near Le Bourget airport, commuting between them in a grass-green Voisin automobile driven by a black chauffeur.

The couple courted notoriety. Their yacht was called Aphrodisiac, and Caresse named her pet whippet Clitoris. Harry attended the annual Quat'z'Arts Ball of artists and models wearing only brown body paint and a necklace of dead pigeons. He also founded his own religion, worshipping the sun. He tattooed the sun on the sole of his right foot and the crucifixion on the left. He and Caresse indulged immoderately in alcohol, drugs and sex. Guests invited to a dinner party might discover them in bed, and be invited to join them. On summer nights, they drove to the Bois de Boulogne with two other couples, parked their cars facing inwards in a circle, and enjoyed six-way sex bathed in the headlights' glare.

As habitual users of opium, called by Harry "Black Idol," the Crosbys were regular clients of Drosso, who ran Paris's most select *fumerie* or opium salon. Harry also frequented the city's brothels, in particular the opulently furnished Le Chabanais, a favorite of crowned heads. He wrote of "the Persian and the Russian and the Turkish and the Japanese and the Spanish rooms, and the bathroom with mirrored walls and mirrored ceilings, and a glimpse of the thirty harlots waiting in the salon [and] the flogging post where men came to flagellate young girls and where others (masochists) came to be flagellated."

Almost as an afterthought, the Crosbys took up the activity for which they would be best remembered—publishing.

When Harry told his father he intended a literary career, the elder Crosby jeered "The idea of you writing poetry as a life work is a joke, and makes everybody laugh." Stung, Harry began socializing with writers in Paris, including Ernest Hemingway and Archibald MacLeish, to whom he showed some of his poetry. Hemingway

Illustration by Alastair for Black Sun Press

was impressed. "Crosby has a wonderful gift of carelessness," he said. "He can just spill the stuff out."

Following the lead of Sylvia Beach at Shakespeare and Company and Robert McAlmon's Contact Press, the Crosbys became publishers. "Ever since I had my first work accepted by one of the little English magazines," wrote Caresse, "and Harry had begun to write sonnnets, we knew that some day we must see our poems in print."

Roger Lescaret, who owned a tiny workshop on rue Cardinale, a short walk from rue de Lille, had never actually done a book. With the Crosbys' unlimited finance, however, it was no great challenge to produce their first collection of poems, *Red Skeletons*. They called the press Editions Narcisse. Ostensibly named after one of Caresse's dogs, it was also an ironic comment on a policy of publishing only the works of its owners. (In mythology, Narcissus fell in love with his own image.) Later, in deference to Harry's sun worship, they retitled their enterprise The Black Sun Press.

The intricacies of book production and design soon seduced Harry and Caresse. Visiting rue Cardinale, a New York bookseller found a scene "like an etching by Rembrandt. Time seemed of little importance. Everything was done leisurely, with infinite care. On proofs that lay about the shop, I noticed the beautiful clarity of the type, the perfect spacing, the wide, elegant margins." When there was no more of their own work to publish, they turned to texts by such writers as D. H. Lawrence, Marcel Proust and Edgar Allan Poe. "The typesetting, the paper choosing, the layout and the binding were all such fun that we went on to greater and more complicated achievement," wrote Caresse.

Their literary idyll couldn't last. His life of excess eroded Harry's stamina and appetite for sensation. He became increasingly jealous of Caresse's lovers, while at the same time pursuing an intense romance with Boston heiress Josephine Rotch. They had met in Venice two years before, and her subsequent marriage had, if anything, only sharpened their passion. Harry's equal in a capacity for sensuality and the urge to self-destruction, Josephine became his most apt pupil.

In November 1929, following the Wall Street crash, Harry and Caresse sailed for New York. A few months before, Harry had wired his father PLEASE SELL $10,000 WORTH OF STOCK. WE HAVE DECIDED TO LEAD A MAD AND EXTRAVAGANT LIFE. While Caresse went on to Boston, Harry remained in New York to defend the cable and be lectured about his profligate ways. Josephine arrived to join him, and was drawn into the vortex of his increasing despair. She wrote a last letter that itemized their shared tastes; caviar, orchids, champagne, the number 13, the color black. It concluded ominously, "Death is our marriage." On December 6, she and Harry met in a studio borrowed from an artist friend. He found them dead the next day. Harry had shot Josephine in the head, then killed himself. He was 31 years old.

transition, the magazine that published Crosby's poems and photographs, ran an obituary by fellow writer Kay Boyle. Her incoherence captured a sense of his fevered life. "There was no one who ever lived more consistently in the thing that was happening then. If he went into retreat, into his own soul he would go, trailing this clattering, jangling universe with him, this ermine-trimmed, this moth-eaten, this wine velvet, the crown jewels on his forehead, the crown of thorns in his hand, into retreat, but never into escape."

SEE IT: THE APARTMENT AND PRINTERY

The building at 19, rue de Lille (5th) where the Crosbys had their apartment still stands. From 1962 to his death in 1976, it was the home of Surrealist painter Max Ernst. The Lescaret printery also still stands at 2, rue Cardinale (6th). Caresse Crosby, though five years older than Harry, outlived him by more than three decades, dying aged 79 in 1970. She continued the Black Sun Press after his death, but with little of his panache. Crosby Continental Editions, a series of paperback reprints and translations of works by Hemingway, Dorothy Parker, Alain-Fournier and Antoine de St.-Exupery, aimed at the American market, was not a success. However, copies of the early Narcisse and Black Sun titles sell for thousands of dollars.

Harry and Caresse Crosby with whippet Clitoris

CHAPTER 25

LOVE FOR SALE: MAISONS CLOSES AND POULES DE LUXE

The 1934 musical *Wonder Bar* presents Paris as a city where sex is as freely sold as cognac and perfume. Gay men dance together while American dowagers, watched by complaisant husbands, tango with gigolos, one of whom sorts through some cards with appropriate phrases before telling his aging partner "You are so sweet. You remind me of my mother."

To Americans shackled by Puritanism, the sensuality of Europe sang a siren song. As France was regarded as "the woman of Europe" and Paris "the woman of France," many foreigners came there as to a sexual resort, ready to wallow in sensation just as, in Rome, they might immerse themselves in art.

Chez Suzy, Brassai, 1931

Maison Closes in Versailles (detail), Eugene Atget, 1921

Before World War I, most American travelers in Europe had been wealthy and well-educated. They either spoke French or had a translator in tow. But the first working-class visitors to 20th-century France, the soldiers of Britain, Australia and the United States fighting World War I, lacked such finesse. Few could say anything more to a French woman than *"Promenez avec moi"* (Walk with me?) or *"Couchez avec moi?"* (Sleep with me?). Most women found such crudeness disgusting, but many did not. Just as the bars and cafés gave up offering French food to soldiers and compromised on fried eggs and frites, women shelved their scruples and learned to flirt in Franglais. By the end of the war, anyone dealing with tourists spoke it fluently.

As servicemen straggled back to the United States and took up their humdrum lives, American journalists, songwriters and filmmakers tantalized them with visions of Paris as a sexual paradise. "*How ya gonna keep 'em down on the farm after they've seen Paree?*" enquired a popular song of 1919. When MGM made *The Big Parade* in 1925, this story of an American soldier falling in love with a French farm girl became the highest-grossing production in Hollywood history. After the introduction of Prohibition in 1920, the prospect of unlimited booze and sex, coupled with the plunging value of the French franc against the dollar, made the lure of Paris irresistible.

Paris's sex workers did their best to accommodate their new clientele. Since the time of Napoleon, prostitution had been almost entirely confined to registered *maisons de tolerance*. Regular medical checks and police supervision controlled disease and crime. While only women could manage a brothel—for a man to do so would make him a pimp, which was illegal—their proprietors behind the scenes often belonged to the highest of high society. Marcel Proust, for instance, owned an interest in two homosexual bordellos.

The best *maisons closes* were as respectable as the "key clubs" of the 1960s; places where gentlemen, aristocrats, even royalty could relax in female company. When a new establishment, The Sphinx, opened in 1931, the mayor of Montparnasse attended, with his wife. They admired the lavish gilded decoration in Egyptian style. The main salon, said one awed client, resembled the lounge of a transatlantic liner, except that most of the women wore nothing but high-heeled shoes. Admission cost 30 francs, for which one could eat in the restaurant, drink at the *bar Americaine*, or enjoy the African-American jazz band. For an additional *pourboire* or tip, they could pass an hour in a mirrored bedroom with one of the establishment's 65 girls. Periodically, they lined up on stage in a streamlined version of the traditional "parade." Bandleader Duke Ellington, on a tour of

Le Sphinx, James Boswell, 1937, Tate Collection

France, was urged to avail himself of all this beauty. Contemplating the line-up, he said, "OK—I'll take the three at the end."

Brassai and Man Ray photographed Le Sphinx, and Alberto Giacometti's sculpture *Four Figurines on a Base* was inspired by a grouping of prostitutes as seen across its polished floor. Henry Miller wrote the text for its publicity brochures, and was paid to steer friends there. One of them was Lawrence Durrell. The author of *The Alexandria Quartet* was in good company. Others included Georges Simenon, Francis Carco and Blaise Cendrars, the painters Moise Kisling, Tsuhugaru Foujita and Jules Pascin, and such performers as Mistinguett, Cary Grant and Humphrey Bogart. Marlene Dietrich used the Sphinx for assignations with one of her lovers, the actress Madeleine Solonge. Celebrities were so common that one of the public phone booths was permanently reserved for the *New York Herald Tribune's* correspondent.

The syndicate of Marseillais businessmen who built the Sphinx was no stranger to organized crime, so the "madame," known as "Martoune," and actually the wife of a part-owner, didn't exclude anyone providing they dressed well and kept the peace. Swindler Serge Stavisky and his ex-model wife Arlette came often, with bodyguard Jo-Jo le Terreur, but her claims that Hitler's mistress Eva Braun visited with friends in 1932, and the Führer himself dropped by on June 23, 1940, are almost certainly false.

Only a few tourists sampled the gourmet sex offered by the *maisons closes*. Most were content with a casual pick up, the erotic equivalent of a hot dog. A 1927 guidebook, published in the U.S., urged the visitor to take an outside table at the Café de la Paix on the Place de l'Opera and "watch the 'Ladies of the Boulevards,' the real Parisians, the gigolos, the male perverts." The same book offers hints on how to meet women; what to pay and when; even the etiquette of visiting a brothel. "The ladies see no harm in you coming merely to inspect them," it explains. "They will parade before you in frankest nudity, and dance with one another in a mirror-walled room, so that of their charms you may miss nothing."

The same book managed a puritanical mixture of lubriciousness and distaste while describing other establishments, such as La Petite Chaumiere ("This is a place where men dress as women: men of a certain degenerate tendency who infest every large city") Le Paradis ("Black men dancing with French girls. Black women dancing with white men") and La Fetiche ("Young ladies dressed as young men.") Not mentioned was Le Monocle, another lesbian club, which

Le Chabanais

required that all clients wear male evening dress, nor the *thés dansants*—afternoon tea dances—at small Montparnasse hotels where young men sat at numbered tables, each furnished with a telephone. Women rang their choice of partner and asked for a dance, after which the couple repaired upstairs.

There were few idiosyncrasies, sexual or otherwise, that Paris could not accommodate. Wondering whether the tribe with which he had spent some time in Africa really gave him human flesh to eat or had merely played a joke on him, American writer William Seabrook bribed a police surgeon to supply flesh from an accident victim and had his housekeeper cook and serve it. He also hired Man Ray to photograph the girls he periodically kept chained up in his house. In 1926, the 22-year-old Salvador Dalí, making his first visit to Paris, went straight from the train station to the city's most select brothel, Le Chabanais. Recognizing that this sexual innocent would rather watch than participate, the manager placed him in a room with a number of peepholes. Dalí left some hours later with, he said, enough images to furnish any sexual fantasy, no matter how detailed. Paris had done it again.

SEE IT: LOVE IS STILL FOR SALE

Le Chabanais (12, rue Chabanais, 2nd) and Le Sphinx (31 blvd Edgar Quinet, 14th) remained open throughout the Nazi occupation of 1940-44, but were reserved for officers only. In 1946, as part of a slightly shamefaced national house-cleaning led by former prostitute and sometime spy Marthe Richard, brothels were declared illegal throughout France on the pretext that their buildings were needed as housing for newlyweds. When most young couples shunned the idea of living in a former whorehouse, they became apartments, in the case of Le Chabanais, or, as with Le Sphinx, were demolished.

There is a lively academic interest in the *maisons closes*, with numerous books on the subject. Introduction and membership cards, the tokens with which the women were paid, and *Guides Roses*, listing establishments and their specialties, are eagerly collected. The Musée de l'Erotisme (72 blvd de Clichy, 18th) devotes a floor to brothel culture, with screenings of the pornographic films often produced and screened there. Most modern prostitution is centered on the internet, though the woods of the Bois de Boulogne remain a favorite haunt. Prostitutes who work from their cars are known as *Amazones*. Police raids in the Bois de Boulogne occasionally drive them onto fashionable avenue Foch (16th), which from time to time is lined with their often expensive automobiles.

Marthe Richard

CHAPTER 26

WASP AND PEAR: THE FITZGERALDS AND THE MURPHYS

When F. Scott Fitzgerald published his fourth novel, *Tender Is the Night,* in 1934, it was already an elegy for a lost time. Its story of Dick and Nicole Diver, an American couple living in the south of France, and the decline of their relationship as Nicole descends into insanity, mirrored not only the personal lives of Scott and Zelda Fitzgerald but also the way in which the indolence and excess of *les années folles* exposed character flaws in even the most well-meaning Americans.

The parallels between the Divers and a real American couple, Gerald and Sara Murphy, were not lost on other expatriates, least of all on the Murphys, who resented being maligned by a man who had been their friend and house guest.

Gerald's family owned Mark Cross, which manufactured and sold luxury leather goods. However, like Harry

The Fitzgeralds celebrating Christmas in Paris, c. 1925

Gerald and Sara Murphy on La Garoupe beach, Antibes, summer 1926

Crosby and a few other wealthy Americans, Murphy shunned business. He volunteered for the army in 1918, but the war ended before he could fight. He studied landscape architecture for a time before deciding to relocate in France. In 1922, he encountered the Cubism of Picasso, Braque and Gris in a Paris gallery. "There was," he wrote later, "a shock of recognition which put me into an entirely new orbit." He told Sara, "That's the kind of painting that I would like to do." Both studied painting with Natalia Gontcharova, and Gerald began to paint the first of only 14 canvases he completed. Meticulously austere macro- or micro- studies of such inanimate subjects as the superstructure of an ocean liner or the interior of a watch, they attracted respect but also charges that they were little better than technical drawings.

The Murphys took to Paris as passionately as the city adopted them. Through Gontcharova, they met Serge Diaghilev. When the sets of the Ballets Russes were damaged in a fire, they helped repaint Leon Bakst's backcloth for *Scheherezade* and Picasso's for *Parade*. Picasso came to assess the repairs, and immediately became their friend. It's suggested that Picasso and Sara became lovers, but she may simply have been one of his numerous infatuations. On the other hand, Picasso did, around this time, paint a number of studies of anonymous women, which might be secret portraits of her.

Fitzgerald dedicated *Tender Is the Night* "To Gerald and Sara —Many Fêtes," a tribute to the couple's delight at a party. To mark the production of Stravinsky's *Les Noces*, the Murphys staged a famous celebration on a barge moored on the Seine. When no flowers could be found to decorate the tables, they created centerpieces of toys. The evening culminated in Stravinsky taking a running dive through one of the giant wreaths created to hang above the festivities. For Count Etienne de Beaumont's Automotive Ball in 1924, Sara created a dress from metal foil, adding outsized driving goggles. Gerald, a tireless show-off, based his costume on a metal breastplate that had to be welded onto his body. He added tights, gauntlets, a helmet that echoed the architecture of Russian constructivist Vladimir Tatlin, and—the final touch—a rearview mirror attached to his shoulder.

In 1923, through his friend the painter Fernand Léger, Murphy was commissioned to design a ballet for the

Ballets Suedoise. To write the music, he chose his Yale classmate Cole Porter. *Within the Quota* tells the story of a Swedish emigrant who goes to America in hopes of becoming a movie star. Murphy's giant backdrop showed the front page of a fake newspaper, *The New York Chicagoan*. Copies of a parody issue were handed out to audiences.

Unexpectedly, the Murphys made their reputation not in Paris but on the Riviera. Until the early 1920s, the only foreigners to visit the Côte d'Azur came from such chill northern countries as Russia. Crown princes and their retinues waited out the winters there, returning to St. Petersburg in April or May, leaving the Riviera to fishermen and the occasional artist. During these sojourns, nobody swam, and everyone, particularly ladies, shunned the sun: a tan showed you were a peasant, forced to work outdoors.

All that changed in November 1920, when the French railways recommenced the Calais-Méditerranée-Express service, suspended since the start of the war in 1914. At Calais, the train picked up passengers arriving from Britain, and carried them in luxury across France, via Paris, to Nice. In 1922, with new steel carriages and a streamlined image, they relaunched the service as *Le Train Bleu—The Blue Train.*

Cole Porter had rented a villa near Antibes. The Murphys visited him, and fell in love with the emptiness of the area. A nearby beach was so little used that a meter of dry seaweed blanketed the sand. They excavated a corner in which to enjoy the sun, and later bought a house nearby, christening it Villa America.

Travel writer Eric Newby credits the Murphys with transforming the Côte d'Azur. "Without realizing it," he wrote, "they had invented a new way of life and

Cole Porter with Gerald's skull cap and Sara's pearls, 1923

the clothes to go with it. Shorts made of white duck, horizontally-striped matelots' jerseys and white work caps bought from sailors' slop shops became a uniform. From now on, the rich, and ultimately everyone else in the northern hemisphere, wanted unlimited sun, the sea, sandy beaches or rocks to dive into it from, and the opportunity to eat *al fresco*." Shortly after, Coco Chanel landed at Antibes from the yacht of her lover the Duke of Westminister, and fashionable Parisians began to imitate her casual clothing and golden tan.

Scott and Zelda Fitzgerald had already discovered the Riviera and rented various houses there, but from May 1926 they became part of a revolving guest list at Villa America that included Pablo Picasso, Man Ray, Cole Porter, John Dos Passos, Dorothy Parker and Jean Cocteau. Intimates recognized tensions within the Murphy marriage and in particular what art critic Alexandra Anderson-Spivy calls Gerald's "narcissistic sense of inner emptiness and his bisexual impulses." To Fitzgerald, life at Villa America seemed ideal material for a book, and he began work on what became *Tender is the Night*.

Jean Cocteau, Pablo Picasso, Igor Stravinsky, and Olga Picasso in Antibes, 1926

Inevitably, the focus of the book widened and the vision of the characters evolved. What had begun as a portrait of the Murphys became increasingly a fictional autobiography. In the novel, Nicole Diver goes insane, as did Zelda, and, like Scott, Dick Diver indulges in a number of affairs. "The book," Fitzgerald said in a letter to the Murphys, "was inspired by Sara and you, and the way I feel about you both and the way you live, and the last part of it is Zelda and me because you and Sara are the same people as Zelda and me." The Murphys strenuously disagreed. In 1962, Sara Murphy said "I didn't like the book when I read it, and I liked it even less on rereading. I reject categorically any resemblance to us or to anyone we knew at any time."

By the time *Tender is the Night* was published, life for the Murphys had deteriorated. Within a few years, both their young sons died. With the stock market crash of 1929, Murphy was forced to return to the U.S. and take over management of Mark Cross, which he ran with great reluctance for the rest of his life. He never painted again, and allowed many of his existing canvases to become lost through neglect. His suffering prompted his friend, the poet Archibald MacLeish, to write *JB*, a modern retelling of the story of Job.

His last painting, *Wasp and Pear*, deceptively tranquil, recalls some brightly colored posters of flowers, fruit and insects he had seen during military training. It shows a smooth green pear in conjunction with a predatory wasp, dull-eyed and malevolent. Is it a metaphor for soft, sweet France at the mercy of foreigners? Or of plump, naive Americans about to suffer the sting of European cynicism? We are left to decide for ourselves. However, in a letter to MacLeish, Murphy wrote of their days at Villa America "What an age of innocence it was, and how beautiful and free!" As his justification for a life spent in the pursuit of pleasure, he proposed an old Spanish proverb: "Living well is the best revenge."

SEE IT: SOUVENIRS OF THE BLUE TRAIN

Tender is the Night, though acknowledged, even by its author, as flawed, remains the most vivid evocation of Villa America and the Murphys. Otherwise, modern France has few reminders of them. All Gerald's seven surviving paintings are in the United States. A few memoirs and biographies evoke the Riviera of their time and a community which, in the words of humorist and then-newspaperman James Thurber, "was full of knaves and rascals, adventurers and imposters, *pochards* and indiscrets, whose ingenious exploits, sometimes in full masquerade costume, sometimes in the nude, were easy and pleasant to record."

Of that Côte d'Azur, the best reminder in Paris is found at the Gare de Lyon railway station (12th). To mark *l'Exposition Universelle* of 1900, the *Compagnie Paris-Lyon-Méditerranée* (PLM) inaugurated a 500-seat restaurant at the station from which trains to the south departed. It was here that the Fitzgeralds and Murphys, Picasso, Chanel, Cocteau, Stravinsky and Diaghilev gathered to share a bottle of Bollinger while they waited to entrain for south. In 1963, the restaurant was renamed, in honor of the PLM's best-known service, *Le Train Bleu*. André Malraux declared it a historical monument in 1972. Forty-one exuberant murals and ceiling paintings celebrate the sun-drenched destinations served by the PLM's trains, and a décor of brass, leather and varnished mahogany evokes the age of luxury rail travel, now returning to France, courtesy of its speedy, silent and comfortable high-speed trains.

Wasp and Pear, Gerald Murphy, 1929, The Museum of Modern Art, New York

The Golden Moments of Paris

WALKING TOURS

I. SEINE LEFT BANK WALK

II. LATIN QUARTER, ST. GERMAIN AND ODEON WALK:
ERNEST HEMINGWAY IN PARIS

III. MONTPARNASSE WALK

IV. TROCADERO WALK

1 Stade Olympique de Colombes
(Chapter 14)
12, rue François Feber

2 Moulin Rouge
(Chapter 14)
82, boulevard de Clichy

3 Folles Bergère
(Chapter 5, 14)
32, rue Richer

4 Coco Chanel's original boutique
(Chapter 7)
31, rue Cambon

5 Ritz Paris
(Chapter 7)
15, place Vendôme

6 Harry's New York Bar
(Chapter 19)
5, rue Danou

7 Site of Le Chabanais
(Chapter 25)
12, rue Chabanais

8 Cole Porter's home
(Chapter 19)
13, rue Monsieur

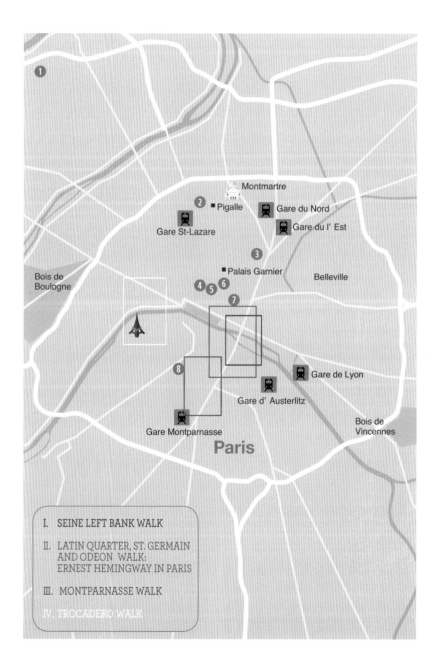

Montmartre

2 ■ Pigalle

Gare du Nord

Gare St-Lazare

Gare du l' Est

3

■ Palais Garnier

Belleville

Bois de
Boulogne

4 5 6

7

Gare de Lyon

8

Gare d' Austerlitz

Bois de
Vincennes

Gare Montparnasse

Paris

I.   SEINE LEFT BANK WALK

II. LATIN QUARTER, ST. GERMAIN
     AND ODEON WALK:
     ERNEST HEMINGWAY IN PARIS

III. MONTPARNASSE WALK

IV. TROCADERO WALK

I. SEINE LEFT BANK WALK

"The quais of the Seine, right and left banks, would be throughout my life my favorite walk," wrote the Surrealist author Philippe Soupault. Few parts of the banks of the Seine as it runs through Paris are without interest, but the stretch between the Pont des Arts, opposite the Louvre, and the Pont de Sully, opposite the end of the Île Saint-Louis, is particularly rich in associations with the 1920s and 1930s.

Leave Metro at Pont Neuf (Line 7). Also called La Monnaie (The Mint), this station serves the Hôtel des Monnaies, which directs the production of currency. Facsimiles of coins and medals and an antique hand press decorate the platforms.

1 La Samaritaine

2 Pont des Arts

3 Hours Press
15, rue Guénégaud

4 Pont Neuf

5 Statue of Henri IV

6 Place Dauphine

7 Home of Yves Montand
and Simone Signoret
15, Place Dauphine

8 Papeteries Gaubert
28, Place Dauphine

9 Quai des Grands-Augustins

10 Desire Caught by the Tail
53b quai des Grands-Augustins

11 Pablo Picasso's studio
7, rue des Grands-Augustins

12 La Perouse
51, quai des Grands-Augustins

13 Cabaret L'Écluse
15, quai des Grands-Augustins

14 Place Saint Michel

15 Theatre de la Huchette
23, rue de la Huchette

16 Brothel Le Panier Fleuri in
The Last Time I Saw Paris
14, rue de la Huchette

17 Caveau de la Huchette
5, rue de la Huchette

18 La Grande Severine
7, rue Saint Séverin

19 Saint Julien le Pauvre
79, rue Galande

20 Shakespeare and Company
37, rue de la Bucherie

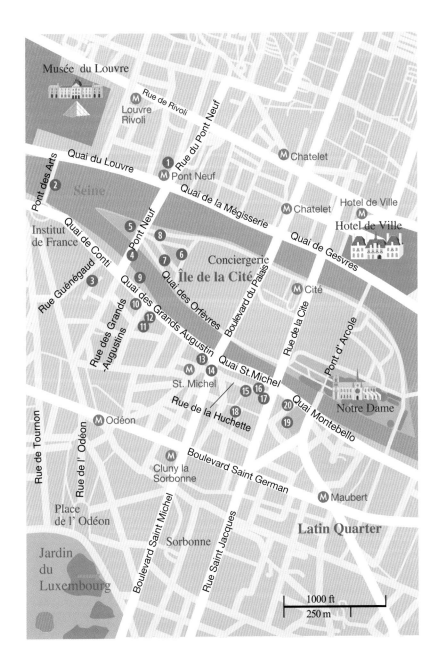

Musée du Louvre

Ⓜ Louvre
Rivoli

Rue de Rivoli

Rue du Pont Neuf

Ⓜ Chatelet

Quai du Louvre

Pont des Arts

❶

Ⓜ Pont Neuf

❷ Seine

Quai de la Mégisserie

Ⓜ Chatelet

Hotel de Ville

Ⓜ Hotel de Ville

Institut
de France

Quai de Conti

❺

Pont Neuf

❽

Quai de Gesvres

Rue Guénégaud

❹

❼ ❻

Conciergerie

Île de la Cité

Ⓜ Cité

❸

Quai des Grands Augustin

❾

Quai des Orfèvres

Boulevard du Palais

Rue de la Cité

❿

Rue des Grands Augustins

⓬

⓫

⓭

Quai St.Michel

Pont d'Arcole

Ⓜ St. Michel

⓮

Rue de Tournon

Rue de l' Odéon

Ⓜ Odéon

⓯ ⓰

⓱

Notre Dame

Rue de la Huchette

⓲

⓴

Quai Montebello

⓳

Boulevard Saint German

Ⓜ Cluny la
Sorbonne

Ⓜ Maubert

Place
de l' Odéon

Boulevard Saint Michel

Sorbonne

Rue Saint Jacques

Latin Quarter

Jardin
du
Luxembourg

| 1000 ft |
| 250 m |

Start:
Métro at Pont Neuf

End:
Métro at Saint Michel

Exit Metro, line 7, Pont Neuf, onto Quai du Louvre.

1. La Samaritaine. This department store complex, named for a well that formerly stood on the site, was once the largest in France. It dominated the area from 1883, swallowing its neighbors and even extending onto the Seine with a floating health spa. Frantz Jourdain's main building, built between 1903 and 1907, was reworked in 1933 by Henri Sauvage, who retained the Art Nouveau staircase and lofty atrium but redesigned the exterior in Art Déco style, using his signature structure of stepped-back tiers. Increasingly dysfunctional, the store closed in 2005. After modernization, it is planned to reopen in 2016 as a hotel and offices.

La Samaritaine, 1929

Turn right and continue on Quai du Louvre. Along this stretch of the river the body of the *L'Inconnue de la Seine* was found.

Quai du Louvre, c.1890

2. Pont des Arts. This metal footbridge, dating from 1804, originally had nine arches, but so many barges collided with the abutments that it was shut down for many years, then rebuilt in 1975 with only seven spans. It is popular with tourists for its views of the river, with artists as a venue for their work, and lately with lovers, who attach padlocks to its railings as tokens of affection.
In Jean Renoir's 1932 film *Boudu sauvé des eaux*, tramp Michel Simon tries to drown himself here. It's the setting for scenes in Claude Chabrol's 1968 *Les Biches* and *Le Fabuleux Destin d'Amélie Poulain* of Jean-Pierre Jeunet. It figures in Philippe Soupault's Surrealist novel *The Last Nights of Paris*. At the Left Bank end, a plaque commemorates the meeting in 1942 of writer Jean Bruller, alias Vercors, and Jacques Lecompte-Boinet of the anti-Nazi resistance in exile. Bruller gave him a copy of his novel *The Silence of the Sea*, the first title published by clandestine Editions de Minuit, to be taken to Charles de Gaulle in London.

Pont des Arts

Turn left and walk along the Quai de Conti, passing the Institut de France and Hôtel des Monnaies. Enter rue Guénégaud.

3. In a storefront at 15, rue Guénégaud, between 1930 and 1934, Nancy Cunard ran the Hours Press, hand-printing limited editions of Samuel Beckett, Pablo Neruda, Laura Riding, Ezra Pound, Richard Aldington and many others. (The street also contains a number of interesting small art galleries, rare book shops, etc.)

rue Guénégaud, Atget, 1908

Return to Quai de Conti. Cross to Pont Neuf. Take left-hand sidewalk onto bridge.

4. Although "Pont Neuf" means "New Bridge," this is Paris's oldest, dating from 1578. It has been repeatedly repaired and reconstructed, but always using the original stones. Leos Carax took advantage of a period of repair to use it as a setting for his 1991 film *Les Amants de Pont Neuf*, but because of production delays, most was shot on a lake near Montpellier. In 1985, Christo used 40,876 meters of fabric and 13,076 meters of cord to wrap the bridge as a work of conceptual art.

Nancy Cunard, 1926

Pont Neuf wrapped by Christo, 198?

5. The point of the island to the left, reached by steps behind the statue of Henri IV, is known as the Vert Galant, one of Henri's nicknames. (A "Green Gallant" is a man who remains virile despite his age.) Jacques de Molay, Grand Master of the Knights Templar, was burned at the stake here in March 1314. More recently, the ashes of Situationist philosopher Guy Debord, formulator of Psychogeography, were thrown into the Seine from this park.

View of the Pont Neuf, 1660s

Cross road to opposite side of bridge and enter rue Henri Robert. Exit into Place Dauphine.

6. The former garden of the Palais de la Cité, now the Palais de Justice or High Court, Place Dauphine is a popular meeting place for strollers, players of *boule*, etc., and a venue for street performers. The office building to the right of the court is part of police headquarters on Quai des Orfevres. Traditionally, one of the high windows was the office of Georges Simenon's Inspector Maigret. Seen from the air, the Île de la Cité and Île Saint Louis resemble a female torso, with Place Dauphine as its

Place Dauphine

Yves Montand and Simone Signoret

Papeteries Gaubert

Quai des Grands-Augustins

First English translation, 1948

7, rue des Grands-Augustins

pubic triangle, leading André Breton to designate it "le sexe de Paris." In his 1927 novel *Nadja*, he made it the home of his mysterious heroine. He called it "one of the most profoundly secluded places I know . . . Whenever I happen to be there, I feel the desire to go somewhere else gradually ebbing out of me. I have to struggle against myself to get free from a gentle, over-insistent, and, finally, crushing embrace."

7. 15, Place Dauphine was for many years the home of actors Yves Montand and Simone Signoret.

8. 28, Place Dauphine houses stationers Papeteries Gaubert. The writer Colette refused to write on anything but their ice-blue paper. They still sell it, and, as in her time, by weight.

Exit Place Dauphine, turn left and return to Left Bank. Turn left and continue along quai des Grands-Augustins.

9. Jean Rhys' 1931 novel *After Leaving Mr. Mackenzie* begins "After she parted from Mr. Mackenzie, Julia Martin went to live in a cheap hotel on the Quai des Grands-Augustins. It looked a lowdown sort of place and the staircase smelt of the landlady's cats, but the rooms were cleaner than you would have expected." She doesn't specify an address but her descriptions could apply to the quai's numerous run-down hotels. The French edition uses the title *Quai des Grands-Augustins*.

10. On the 4th floor at 53b quai des Grands-Augustins, on March 19, 1944, Surrealist writer Michel Leiris staged a reading, directed by Albert Camus, of Pablo Picasso's only play *Desire Caught by the Tail*, performed by Jean-Paul Sartre, Dora Maar, Simone de Beauvoir and the author.

Turn right into rue des Grands-Augustins.

11. From 1936 until 1946, the loft at the top of 7, rue des Grands-Augustins was Pablo Picasso's studio. So large that, in the words of photographer Brassai, "one had the

234

impression of being inside a ship," the attic of this 17th century building gave him the space to paint his 1937 *Guernica*, 25 feet long by 11 feet high.

Pablo Picasso's studio

The building housed a number of writers during the 19th century, including Honoré de Balzac, who set his story "The Unknown Masterpiece" there. During the 1930s, it was used by the Surrealists, by the October 1932 group of poet Jacques Prevert, and, between 1932 and 1936, by the theater group of Jean-Louis Barrault.

Return Quai des Grands-Augustins.

12. At 51, quai des Grands-Augustins is the famous—and famously expensive—restaurant Lapérouse, popular with George Sand, Guy de Maupassant, Émile Zola and Victor Hugo. Formerly a brothel, it retains its original architecture of small private rooms for discreet liaisons, well recreated in Henri-Georges Clouzot's 1947 film *Quai des Orfevres*, where jealous husband Bernard Blier interrupts wife Suzy Delair as she dines with sordid publisher Charles Dullin.

Lapérouse

Cabaret L'Ecluse

13. Between 1951 and 1975, 15, quai des Grands-Augustins was the site of the tiny Cabaret L'Écluse, one of the performance venues that won the Latin Quarter its postwar reputation for bohemian entertainment. Jacques Brel, Marcel Marceau and Philippe Noiret performed here.

14. Place St. Michel. Regarded as the gate to the Left Bank, this wide intersection is dominated by Francisque-Joseph Duret's fountain and the statue of the Archangel Michael trampling the devil. After World War II, the fountain was rededicated as a monument to French citizens who died resisting Nazi occupation. The square and boulevard St. Michel ("'boul'Mich") saw pitched battles during the 1968 student revolution when trees along the thoroughfare were felled to create barricades.

Statue of Archangel Michael

Place St. Michel, c. 1900

Cross boulevard St. Michel and enter rue de la Huchette.

The Latin Quarter was originally so called because of the medieval religious schools that clustered here. In modern times, the nightclubs and cabarets that took over its shopfronts and cellars made the term "Latin Quarter" synonymous with bohemianism.

Theatre de la Huchette

15. Since 1957, the tiny 85-seat Theatre de la Huchette (23, rue de la Huchette) has presented only plays by Eugene Ionesco. More than 1.5 million people have seen its double bill of *The Lesson* and *The Bald Prima Donna*.

14, rue de la Huchette

16. American expatriate Elliott Paul, sometime editor of the magazine *transition* and intimate of Gertrude Stein and James Joyce, celebrated rue de la Huchette in his 1942 novel *The Last Time I Saw Paris*. In the book, the building at 14, rue de la Huchette, marked by a letter "Y" chiseled into the stone, housed the brothel Le Panier Fleuri—The Flower Basket.

Caveau de la Huchette

17. Caveau de la Huchette (5, rue de la Huchette) is a jazz venue in a medieval cellar. Among those who have performed here are Lionel Hampton, Harry "Sweets" Edison, "Memphis Slim" and Art Blakey's Jazz Messengers. Today a house group plays boogie and swing, suitable for dancing.

Caveau de la Huchette, 1957

Turn right, cross the square in front of the Eglise Saint Séverin and enter rue Saint Séverin.

Maurice Girodias (standing) & Peter Orlovsky at the nightclub, 1961

18. From 1959 to 1964, 7, rue Saint Séverin housed La Grande Severine, the arts and performance complex of Maurice Girodias, owner of the Olympia Press and publisher of Nabokov's *Lolita*, Samuel Beckett's *Watt and Molloy*, and numerous works of pornography. Chez Vodka specialized in Russian music, performers at the Brazilian-themed La Batacuda included Marpessa Dawn, star of the film *Black Orpheus*, and in the Blues-Bar and basement Jazzland, Ornette Coleman and Cecil Taylor played. In 1964, Girodias challenged censorship by staging an adaptation of the Marquis de Sade's *La Philosophie dans le boudoir*. The production was seen by actress Catherine Deneuve, director Roger Vadim and novelist Romain

Gary, but as Girodias had no license to present theater, he was forced to shut down.

Exit onto rue du Petit-Pont and cross to rue Galande.

19. The church of Saint Julien le Pauvre (Saint Julien the Poor) at 79, rue Galande is one of the oldest in Paris. On April 14, 1921, a group including André Breton, Tristan Tzara, Philippe Soupault and Francis Picabia stood in front of it and mocked passers-by in what was called a "Dada Excursion." They also offered guided tours of the nearby morgue. The event, regarded as a failure by Breton, spurred him to break with Dada and launch Surrealism.

St. Julien le Pauvre

Dada Excursion, 1921

Continue to the riverbank and turn left into rue de la Bucherie.

20. Shakespeare and Company at 37, rue de la Bucherie, is Paris's largest and most popular English-language bookshop. Opened in 1951 by George Whitman as Le Mistral, it became Shakespeare and Company after the death of Sylvia Beach in 1964. Portions of the lending library from the original store on rue de l'Odéon are housed in an upstairs reading room. During the 1960s, the shop hosted such writers as Lawrence Durrell and provided a haven for such Beat Generation figures as Gregory Corso, Gary Snyder, Lawrence Ferlinghetti and Allen Ginsberg, some of whom slept on the floor of the office next door (now its Rare Book Room.) The shop figures in numerous books and films, including Richard Linklater's *Before Sunset* (2004) and Woody Allen's *Midnight in Paris* (2011).

Shakespeare and Company

Before Sunset, 2004

Return Saint Michel metro stop.

II. LATIN QUARTER, ST. GERMAIN AND ODEON WALK: ERNEST HEMINGWAY IN PARIS

Except for such Surrealists as Louis Aragon, Philippe Soupault and André Breton, who each devoted a book to his promenades, no Paris-based writer was so strenuous a pedestrian as Ernest Hemingway. This tour includes a few of the numerous sites associated with his seven years in Paris.

1 Rue Mouffetard

2 Café Delmas
2-4, Place Contrescarpe

3 Hemingway's apartment
74, rue Cardinal-Lemoine

4 Hemingway's office
39, rue Descartes

5 Jardins du Luxembourg

6 Gertrude Stein and Alice Toklas's apartment
27, rue de Fleurus

7 Gerald and Sara Murphy's apartment
14, rue Guynemer

8 Scott and Zelda Fitzgerald's apartment
58, rue de Vaugirard

9 Musée d' Luxembourg
19, rue de Vaugirard

10 Hemingway and Pauline Pfeiffer's apartment
6, rue Férou

11 Café des Deux Magots
6, Place Jean Paul Sartre/Simone de Beauvoir

12 Brasserie Lipp
151, boulevard St. Germain

13 Café Pre aux Clercs
30, rue Bonaparte

14 Hôtel d'Angleterre (Jacob)
44, rue Jacob

15 Le Comptoir des Saints-Pères (Michaud's)
29, rue des Saints-Pères

16 Robert McAlmon's Contact Press
8, rue de l'Odéon

17 Original Shakespeare and Company bookshop
12, rue de l'Odéon

18 Sylvia Beach and Adrienne Monnier's apartment
18, rue de l'Odéon

A La Closerie des Lilas
171, boulevard du Montparnase

B Michael and Sarah Stein's apartment
58, rue Madame

C Café de Flore
172, boulevard St. Germain

D Café Procope
13, rue Ancienne Comédie

E Harry and Caresse's apartment
19, rue de Lille

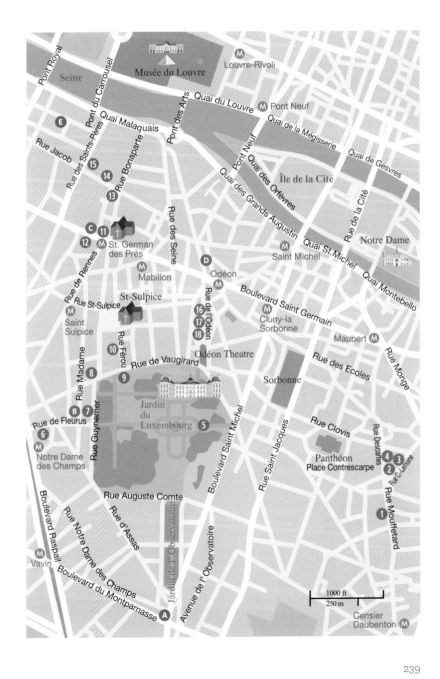

Pont Royal

Seine

Musée du Louvre

Louvre-Rivoli Ⓜ

Pont du Carrousel

Quai Malaquais

Quai du Louvre

Ⓜ **Pont Neuf**

Rue des Saints-Pères

Pont des Arts

Quai de la Mégisserie

Ⓔ

Rue Jacob

Quai Neuf

Quai de Gesvres

⑮

Rue Bonaparte

⑭

Quai des Orfèvres

Île de la Cité

⑬

Quai des Grands Augustin

Rue de la Cité

Rue des Seine

Ⓒ ⑪

Notre Dame

⑫ Ⓜ **St. German**
des Prés

Ⓓ

Quai St. Michel

Ⓜ
Saint Michel

Notre Dame

Rue de Rennes

Ⓜ
Mabillon

Odéon
Ⓜ

Quai Montebello

St-Sulpice

Rue des Seine

Boulevard Saint Germain

Rue St-Sulpice

⑯

Cluny-la
Sorbonne

Maubert Ⓜ

Ⓜ
Saint
Sulpice

Rue Férou

⑰

Rue de l'Odéon

⑱

Rue Monge

Rue Madame

⑩

Odéon Theatre

Rue des Ecoles

Rue de Vaugirard

⑧

⑨

Sorbonne

Jardin
du
Luxembourg

Boulevard Saint Michel

Rue Clovis

Ⓑ ⑦

⑤

Rue Guynemer

Rue de Fleurs

Rue Saint Jacques

Panthéon
Place Contrescarpe

Rue Descartes

Ⓑ ⑦

⑥

Ⓐ④③

Ⓜ
Notre Dame
des Champs

Rue C. Lemoine

②

Rue Auguste Comte

Rue Mouffetard

Boulevard Raspail

Rue Notre Dame des Champs

Rue d'Assas

Jardin de l' Observatoire

①

Ⓜ
Vavin

Avenue de l' Observatoire

1000 ft
250 m

Boulevard du Montparnasse

Ⓐ

Censier
Daubenton Ⓜ

Start:
Métro at Censier Daubenton

End:
Métro at Odéon

Rue Mouffetard, 1896

Café Delmas at Pl. Contrescarpe

74, rue Cardinal-Lemoine

Hemingway and Hadley with
Parisian expatriate friends

Exit Metro at Censier Daubenton (Line 7).

1. Rue Mouffetard. On weekends in particular, this is an archetypal Paris food and vegetable market, narrow, slippery underfoot in wet weather but brightly lit, filled with jostling shoppers and sellers shouting bargains. Hemingway writes of "that wonderful narrow crowded market street which led into the Place Contrescarpe." In his time, the neighborhood was rougher and poorer. In 1928, George Orwell lived off Mouffetard on rue de Pot de Fer (which he called rue de Coq d'Or) while writing *Down and Out in Paris and London*. "Quarrels, and the desolate cries of street hawkers, and the shouts of children chasing orange-peel over the cobbles, and at night loud singing and the sour reek of the refuse carts, made up the atmosphere of the street . . . Poverty is what I'm writing about and I had my first contact with poverty in this slum."

2. Café Delmas, 2-4, Place Contrescarpe. This was formerly the Café des Amateurs, described by Hemingway as the "cesspool of the rue Mouffetard . . . a sad, evilly run café where the drunkards of the quarter crowded together and I kept away from it because of the smell of dirty bodies and the sour smell of drunkenness." He describes flower sellers dyeing their carnations and prostitutes living above the *bal musette* or dance hall where they worked. All the same, "there never was another part of Paris that he loved like that, the sprawling trees, the old white plastered houses painted brown below, the long green of the autobus in that round square, the purple flower dye upon the paving."

3. From 1922 to 1926, Hemingway lived here (74, rue Cardinal-Lemoine) on the third floor, "the poorest of addresses," with his first wife, Hadley, and their son. As usual at the time, the apartment had no hot water and all tenants shared the squat or "Turkish" toilet on the landing.

Turn left up rue Cardinal-Lemoine, right into rue Clovis and right into rue Descartes.

4. On the top floor of a residential hotel at 39, rue Descartes, Hemingway rented a work room in, coincidentally, the building where poet Paul Verlaine died in 1896. A large plaque commemorates the Verlaine association and a smaller one, with inaccurate dates, Hemingway's sojourn here. "The fireplace drew well in the room and it was warm and pleasant to work. I brought mandarins and roasted chestnuts to the room in paper packets and peeled and ate the small tangerine-like oranges and threw their skins and spat their seeds in the fire when I ate them and the roasted chestnuts when I was hungry."

Return to rue Clovis, descend to Place du Pantheon, then rue Soufflot to rue de Medicis.

Cross rue de Medicis and enter Luxembourg Gardens.

5. Jardins du Luxembourg. Though he is sometimes described as "loitering" in these gardens, Hemingway probably did so only when he and Hadley took their son for a walk on weekends. (He is also unlikely, as some suggest, to have grabbed and strangled pigeons for the pot, they being wary and Hemingway notoriously maladroit.) More likely, he detoured across the gardens as a short cut, and to avoid restaurants with their tantalizing savory smells. "You saw and smelled nothing to eat from the Place de l'Observatoire to the rue de Vaugirard."

(Optional: turn left and walk south to the top of the Luxembourg Gardens. Exit onto boulevard du Montparnasse.
La Closerie des Lilas, 171, boulevard du Montparnase. This restaurant was formerly a *relais* or coach stop on the main road to Fontainebleu. By Hemingway's time, it had become a modest café with a terrace sheltered by lilac trees. When Hemingway lived in the area, it was his favorite place to work. "The only decent café in our neighborhood was La Closerie des Lilas, and it was one of the best cafés in Paris. It was warm in the winter and the terrace was lovely in the spring and fall." He wrote some of his early stories here, including "Big Two Hearted

39, rue Descartes

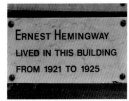
Hemingway wrote here, 1922-23

Jardins du Luxembourg

La Closerie des Lilas

La Closerie des Lilas, c. 1920

River," and part of *The Sun Also Rises*, portions of which are set in the café. Descend Luxembourg gardens and exit left onto rue Guynemer.)

Exit gardens at rue Guynemer and enter rue de Fleurus.

27, rue de Fleurus

6. Gertrude Stein and Alice Toklas shared an apartment at 27, rue de Fleurus. Hemingway often dropped in to chat. "It was easy to get into the habit of stopping in at 27, rue de Fleurus for warmth and the great pictures and the conversation." Stein and Hemingway, with some help from Toklas, who resented their friendship, finally fell out in an argument about the relative literary merits of Sherwood Anderson, whose work Hemingway parodied in his novel *The Torrents of Spring*.

14, rue Guynemer

Return to rue Guynemer, descend to rue de Vaugirard.

7. From 1927 to 1929, Gerald and Sara Murphy, partial models for Dick and Nicole Diver in F. Scott Fitzgerald's *Tender is the Night*, owned an apartment in this exceptional Art Déco building (14, rue Guynemer), designed by Michel Roux-Spitz. Earlier in the 1920s, the bisexual Gerald belonged to the gay circle surrounding Étienne de Beaumont and Cole Porter, with whom he collaborated on the ballet *Within the Quota*.

58, rue de Vaugirard

8. At 58, rue de Vaugirard, from April to October 1928, Scott and Zelda Fitzgerald rented an apartment belonging to Gerald and Sara Murphy. Hemingway visited them there, and was critical of Scott's insistence on having a fashionable address. It's sometimes suggested that it was here they had the famous exchange—"The rich are very different from you and me, Ernest," to which Hemingway replied, "Yes, they have more money." (In fact, a similar conversation appears in a much earlier Fitzgerald story.)

Scott and Zelda Fitzgerald

Continue on rue de Vaugirard.

A Picture gallery at the Musée du Luxembourg, French School, 1883-85

9. In Hemingway's time, this pavilion, the Musée du Luxembourg at 19, rue de Vaugirard (joined to the Palais

de Luxembourg by the Orangerie) housed part of the national collection of Impressionist painting, in particular the work of Paul Cézanne. On the advice of Gertrude Stein, Hemingway studied painting to improve his writing, and admired Cézanne in particular. He visited this gallery often. "I learned to understand Cézanne much better and to see truly how he made landscapes when I was hungry. I used to wonder if he were hungry too when he painted; but I thought possibly it was only that he had forgotten to eat. It was one of those unsound but illuminating thoughts you have when you have been sleepless or hungry. Later I thought Cézanne was probably hungry in a different way."

Cross rue de Vaugirard to rue Férou.

6, rue Férou

Pauline Pfeiffer

10. In the summer of 1926, Hemingway left Hadley and his son and moved in with Pauline Pfeiffer at 6, rue Férou into a large apartment belonging to her wealthy uncle Gus, who owned Hudnut perfumes. While there, he worked on *A Farewell to Arms*, which is dedicated to Gus Pfeiffer, and socialized with, among others, poet Archibald MacLeish and Canadian writer Morley Callaghan, with whom he boxed.

Descend rue Férou, cross Place Saint Sulpice, turn left on rue Saint Sulpice, continue to rue de Rennes, turn right on rue de Rennes to join boulevard Saint Germain at Place Jean Paul Sartre/Simone de Beauvoir (formerly Place Saint-Germain des Prés.)

Saint Sulpice

11. For more than a century, the Café des Deux Magots at 6, Place Jean Paul Sartre/Simone de Beauvoir has been popular with Paris literati. In the 1960s, when Algerian separatists bombed Sartre's apartment and he moved out of the area, he switched to upstairs at the Café de Flore. When Hemingway lived on nearby rue Jacob during his first days in the city, he probably patronized it, though he makes no reference to the fact.

Café des Deux Magots

Cross boulevard Saint Germain.

Brasserie Lipp

12. Hemingway was a regular client for lunch at this former brewery, Brasserie Lipp at 151, boulevard Saint Germain, in particular enjoying *cervelas* sausage on cold boiled potatoes dressed with olive oil, washed down with Lipp's own beer, at that time brewed in the basement.

Cross boulevard Saint Germain and descend rue Bonaparte to rue Jacob.

Café Pre aux Clercs

13. At the intersection with rue Bonaparte, the Café Pre aux Clercs was a Hemingway hangout. Although some have suggested the incident took place at Michaud's (see below), it was probably here, in the basement bathroom, that he had his notorious encounter with F. Scott Fitzgerald, described in the episode "A Matter of Measurements" in *A Moveable Feast*, when the former asked him to examine his penis and tell him if it was, as Zelda had charged, too small to satisfy a real woman.

Continue left on rue Jacob.

Hôtel d'Angleterre

14. On their first night in Paris in December 1921, Hemingway and Hadley stayed in Room 14 at the Hôtel Jacob (now Hôtel d'Angleterre) at 44, rue Jacob. A small display in the lobby commemorates the fact.

Continue on rue Jacob to rue de Saints-Pères.

29, rue des Saints-Pères

15. Le Comptoir des Saints-Pères at 29, rue des Saints-Pères was formerly Michaud's, an expensive restaurant in this otherwise modest district. James Joyce and his family ate there often. Indignant on behalf of Sylvia Beach, who was financially supporting Joyce, Hemingway commented "Joyce has written a most goddam wonderful book (*Ulysses*). Meantime the report is that he and all his family are starving, but you can find the whole Celtic crew of them in Michaud."

Joyce family, 1924

Reverse direction of rue Jacob until it terminates in rue de Seine. Turn right, then left on boulevard Saint Germain and right on rue de l'Odéon.

Rue de l'Odéon

16. 8, rue de l'Odéon formerly housed Robert McAlmon's Contact Press, which published Hemingway's first book, *Three Stories and Ten Poems*.

17. 12, rue de l'Odéon is the site of the original Shakespeare and Company bookshop, which provided Hemingway with his first literary contacts in Paris. "She was kind, cheerful and interested," he wrote of the proprietor, Sylvia Beach, "and loved to make jokes and gossip. No one that I ever knew was nicer to me."

18. On the 4th floor at 18, rue de l'Odéon, Sylvia Beach shared an apartment with her companion Adrienne Monnier from 1922 to 1937. As his first act on entering Paris in 1944, ahead of the main allied armies, Hemingway "liberated" Odéon, before moving on to the Ritz Hotel for martinis.

Descend rue de l'Odéon and rejoin Metro at Odéon (Lines 4 and 10.)

Robert McAlmon

Shakespeare and Company, 1919

18, rue de l'Odeon

III. MONTPARNASSE WALK

Montparnasse is named for Mount Parnassus, the Greek mountain on which the muses were said to live. Originally settled by Italian stoneworkers who executed the façades for Haussmann's rebuilt Paris in the 1850s, it earned its name from the number of artists who made it their home. Heavy-drinking painters and promiscuous models gave it a reputation for bohemianism. This persisted well after the artists and models had moved on, encouraged by the bar and café owners who catered to the tourists who flocked there in the 1920s, and continue to do so.

1 La Rotonde
105, boulevard du Montparnasse

2 Statue of Honoré de Balzac

3 Café Select
99, boulevard du Montparnasse

4 La Coupole
102, boulevard du Montparnasse

5 Le Dôme
108, boulevard du Montparnasse

6 Tsuguharu Foujita's apartment
5, rue Delambre

7 The New Review office
8, rue Delambre

8 Isadora Duncan's apartment
9, rue Delambre

9 Auberge de Venise (Le Dingo)
10, rue Delambre

10 Rosebud Bar
11bis, rue Delambre

11 Hôtel Lenox (Man Ray's studio)
15, rue Delambre

12 Simone de Beauvoir's home
33, rue Delambre

13 Hôtel Delambre
35, rue Delambre

14 Place Joséphine Baker

15 Le Maldoror
60, boulevard Edgar Quinet

16 Site of the Le Sphinx
31, boulevard Edgar Quinet

17 Le Monocle
14, boulevard Edgar Quinet

18 Montparnasse Cemetery

19 Hôtel L'Aiglon
232, boulevard Raspail

20 Man Ray's apartment & studio
31bis, rue Campagne Première

21 Hôtel Istria
29, rue Campagne Première

22 The Passage d'Enfer

23 Eugene Atget's studio
17bis, rue Campagne Première

24 Cité des Artistes
9, rue Campagne Première

25 Site of Chez Rosalie
3, rue Campagne Première

26 Site of Jockey Club

27 Closerie des Lilas
171, boulevard du Montparnasse

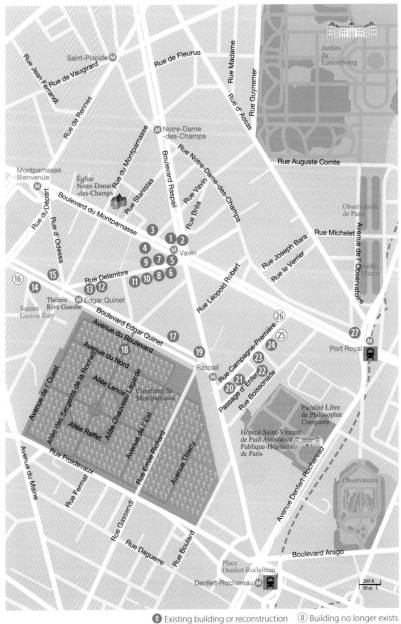

Existing building or reconstruction   Building no longer exists

Start:
Métro at Vavin

End:
PER at Port Royal

Exit the Metro at Vavin (Line 4) at the intersection of boulevard du Montparnasse and boulevard Raspail.

1. On the corner nearest the Metro exit, la Rotonde, opened in 1910, is one of the most famous Paris cafés, patronized by expatriates of every nationality, from Henry Miller and Pablo Picasso to Khalil Gibran and Vladimir Ilyich Lenin. It was a particular favorite of the Hispanic and Catalan community. During the 1920s, Spanish philosopher Miguel de Unamuno convened a daily *peña* or forum, attended by Luis Buñuel, Juan Castanayer and Ismael de la Serna.
Cross to island in the middle of boulevard Raspail on the downhill side.

La Rotonde

Kisling, Pâquerette, Picasso, 1916

2. Auguste Rodin's statue of novelist Honoré de Balzac has stood here since 1939. Rodin completed a plaster version in 1891, but the commissioning body, the Société des Gens de Lettres, refused to accept it, claiming the cloaked figure didn't look human. It wasn't cast in bronze until 22 years after Rodin's death, when it was immediately acknowledged as one of his greatest works, and a milestone in modern sculpture.
Return to boulevard du Montparnasse and continue west.

Balzac by Auguste Rodin

3. At no. 99, on the corner with rue Vavin, is the Café Select. Opened in 1925 , it was the first of the great cafés to remain open all night, and became popular with what Hemingway called "ladies of both sexes." In 1929, poet Hart Crane spent six days in jail after a drunken fight with waiters over the bill. It also was a favorite of Henry Miller, filmmaker Luis Buñuel, and of political radical Emma Goldman. African American author James Baldwin wrote most of his novel *Giovanni's Room* here.

Cross boulevard du Montparnasse.

Café Select

4. At no. 102, the café/restaurant La Coupole (The Cupola) opened in 1927, and combined café, restaurant, a basement dance hall and an "American bar," which served the cocktails tourists demanded. Defying André Breton's prohibition on the Surrealists visiting Montparnasse,

Louis Aragon was a regular. He met his wife Elsa Triolet here in 1928, and in 1929 was introduced by Man Ray to Salvador Dalì and Luis Buñuel, who invited him to view their film *Un Chien Andalou*, and decide whether it was truly Surrealist. La Coupole was also patronized by Picasso, Jean Cocteau's novelist lover Raymond Radiguet, Foujita, Kisling, Giacometti, Zadkine and model Alice Prin, aka Kiki of Montparnasse. Originally two stories, the building was rebuilt in 1986, adding offices and apartments, though the restaurant retains its noisy charm, as well as the original Art Déco floor tiling. The columns are also original, by students of Henri Matisse and Fernand Léger, who had studios on nearby rue Notre Dame des Champs.

Walk back along boulevard du Montparnasse towards boulevard Raspail.

5. On the corner, the Dôme dates from 1898. In exile before the 1917 revolution, Lenin and Trotsky were regulars, as were Henry Miller, Man Ray and Samuel Beckett. Hemingway's *A Moveable Feast* describes an evening spent with the painter Jules Pascin at the Dôme. It became so intimately associated with the expat community that cab drivers with passengers too drunk to remember their addresses would deliver them to the Dôme, assuming someone there would recognize them. The terrace, once open to the street, is now enclosed, and the café itself has become a seafood restaurant.
Make a sharp right turn into rue Delambre.

6. Japanese painter Leonard Tsuguharu Foujita had his studio at no. 5 from 1917 until 1926, where he entertained Amedeo Modigliani, Jules Pascin, Chaim Soutine, and Fernand Léger. Among his models was Alice Prin, who had become the model and lover of Man Ray.

7. At no. 8, between 1930 and 1932, Samuel Putnam edited the five issues of the influential "little magazine" *The New Review*. Ezra Pound was associate editor. It published numerous expatriate writers, including Henry Miller, Samuel Beckett and Robert McAlmon.

La Coupole

La Coupole, c.1930

The Dôme

Foujita, 1917

Ezra Pound, John Quinn, Ford Madox Ford, and James Joyce, 1923

Duncan & husband Yesenin, 1923

8. From 1926, dancer Isadora Duncan, then in her late forties, lived at no. 9. No longer able to command large sums for her performances, she famously complained "I don't know where the next bottle of Champagne is coming from." She gave private lessons to, among others, her neighbor Foujita. In 1927, she would die dramatically in Nice, her neck broken when her scarf caught in the wheel of an automobile.

The site of Le Dingo bar

9. No. 10, now the Auberge de Venise, is the site of the former bar Le Dingo (from French slang: *dingue*, "crazy"). In April 1925, Hemingway and F. Scott Fitzgerald met here for the first time. Other clients included Sinclair Lewis, Sherwood Anderson, John Dos Passos, Ezra Pound, Henry Miller and Thornton Wilder.

Sartre & de Beauvoir

10. The Rosebud Bar at 11 bis was frequented in 1937 by both Jean-Paul Sartre and Simone de Beauvoir, who lived separately in hotels on the street.

11. At no. 15, at the Hôtel Lenox (formerly Grand Hôtel des Écoles), Tristan Tzara, founder of the Dada movement, lived in 1921. At the same time, Man Ray occupied a room as his first studio in Paris. Henry Miller met Alfred Perles here in May 1925, and "a friendship was begun which was to color the entire period of my stay in France." The two men later shared an apartment, an episode that inspired Miller's *Quiet Days in Clichy*. Miller also lived here with his wife June from 1928 to 1930.

15, rue Delambre

12. Simone de Beauvoir lived at no. 33, Hôtel des Bains, in 1937.

Hôtel des Bains

13. Plaques in the entrance to the Hôtel Delambre at no. 35, formerly the Hôtel des Écoles (not to be confused with the Grand Hôtel des Écoles at no. 15), note that painter Paul Gauguin lived here in 1891 and André Breton, founder of Surrealism, in 1920-1921 after giving up his medical studies. Disliking the triviality of Montparnasse, Breton moved to less pretentious Montmartre. In 1927, the hotel was home to the young British painter Francis Bacon.

14. Place Joséphine Baker, at the intersection of rue Poinsot, rue Jolivet and boulevard Edgar Quinet, is one of two sites dedicated to the African-American star of the Revue Negre (the other is a public swimming pool in the 13th arrondissement). Baker had no association with this location, which was probably chosen because of its proximity to the theaters of rue de la Gaité.

Hôtel Delambre (right)

Enter boulevard Edgar Quinet, which runs along the side of the Montparnasse Cemetery.

Place Joséphine Baker

15. On February 14, 1930, the dance hall Le Maldoror at no. 60 was the site of a famous Surrealist attack. Breton, objecting to the use of a name associated with Isidore Ducasse, self-styled Comte de Lauréamont, a Surrealist hero and author of *Songs of Maldoror*, demanded the proprietor change it. When he refused, Breton, swinging a lead-weighted cane, led André Thirion, René Char and others in smashing glassware and ripping up linen.

Joséphine Baker, 1934

16. No. 31 was the former site of the brothel Le Sphinx. (The original building has been demolished.) Opened in 1931, Le Sphinx was the most lavish of Paris's so-called *maisons de tolerance* (indicating that it operated with the approval of the authorities). Guests at the opening included the mayor of Montparnasse and his wife. The Egyptian décor set new standards in opulence. It was also the first building in Paris to be air-conditioned. Henry Miller wrote the text for its promotional brochures, and took payment "in trade," plus a bonus for each new client introduced. Novelist Lawrence Durrell recalled spending "fabulous hours with Henry Miller at the Sphinx." Other celebrity visitors included band-leader Duke Ellington. Like all France's brothels, Le Sphinx was shut down in 1946 as part of a morality drive spearheaded by Marthe Richard, famous as a spy during World War I and herself a former prostitute.

Isidore Ducasse (1846-1870)

Le Sphinx

17. From the early 1930s to 1940, the lesbian club Le Monocle occupied the basement at no. 14. Cross-dressers were asked to wear male evening dress; monocles were optional. Photographer Brassai, who documented the

Le Monocle

Montparnasse Cemetery

Sartre & de Beauvoir's grave

Hôtel L'Aiglon

Buñuel & Deneuve, 1969

club in his 1932 book *Paris de Nuit*, wrote "The boss, Lulu of Montparnasse, the barmaid, the tarts, waitresses, not forgetting the hat check girl, all dressed as men."

Cross to Montparnasse Cemetery.

18. Created from farmland in 1824, this is the resting place of numerous figures from literature, politics and the arts. These include the shared grave of Jean-Paul Sartre and Simone de Beauvoir, the plain black marble slab of Samuel Beckett, Man Ray's monument with its reticent epitaph "Unconcerned, but not Indifferent," the grave of Alice Prin, aka Kiki of Montparnasse, and the photograph-decorated grave of singer Serge Gainsbourg. Gays or personalities of gay interest buried here include actress Delphine Seyrig, camp icon Maria Montez, Pierre Louys, author of the spuriously *Sapphic Songs of Bilitis*, photographer Gisele Freund, and film director Jacques Demy.

Signs at the main entrances indicate the general position of most celebrity graves, but you may need to ask one of the attendants for specific directions.

Exit Cemetery onto boulevard Edgar Quinet and continue towards boulevard Raspail.

19. At 232 boulevard Raspail, at the corner of boulevard Edgar Quinet, stands the Hôtel L'Aiglon. Film director Luis Buñuel lived here in the 1960s, during the making of *Diary of a Chambermaid*, *Belle de Jour* and *The Milky Way*. His windows gave a view of the cemetery, which he claimed to find consoling, but which spooked actresses he invited there, in particular Catherine Deneuve. In June 1961, after terrorists bombed the apartment on rue Bonaparte that he shared with his mother, Jean-Paul Sartre moved to Montparnasse, and installed his mother in this hotel, by coincidence next door to Buñuel.

Cross boulevard Raspail, turn right, then left into rue Campagne Première.

Many artists of the late 19th and early 20th century lived on this street, which was convenient to their studios on the other side of boulevard du Montparnasse, notably on rue Campagne Première.

31 bis rue Notre Dame des Champs

20. In 1926, Man Ray moved into this distinctive building at no. 31 bis, designed by André Arfvidson in 1911, with striking ceramics by Alexandre Bigot. It became Ray's primary apartment and studio, though he kept another studio on rue Val de Grace. He lived here with Alice Prin until 1929, and thereafter for three years with Lee Miller, with whom he developed the Rayograph process.

Hôtel Istria

21. Picabia, Duchamp, Kisling, Man Ray and Kiki de Montparnasse were among the artists who patronized the modest Hôtel Istria at no. 29. A plaque prominently placed on the façade lists a number of them.

22. The Passage d'Enfer (Hell's Passage) is a short lane that makes an abrupt right-hand turn to rejoin boulevard Raspail. In 1871, Arthur Rimbaud lived in a room here, paid for by his lover Paul Verlaine. The Passage reveals some unusual features of Arfvidson's architecture for 31 bis, including ventilated serveries designed to keep food cool in that pre-refrigerator era.

Passage d'Enfer

23. No. 17 bis was formerly the home and studio of pioneering photographer Eugene Atget, who meticulously documented the streets and buildings of old Paris. This building became famous after 1927 as the site of Stanley Hayter's print-making studio Atelier 17. Miro, Dalì, Giacometti, Ernst, Picasso, Lipschitz and Jackson Pollock learned the principles of etching and lithography here.

Eugene Atget

24. After the Universal Exposition of 1889, some materials were salvaged to create a Cité des Artistes of 100 tiny studios on this site at no. 9. Among those who occupied them were Amadeo Modigliani, James McNeill Whistler and Giorgio de Chirico.

Cité des Artistes

25. Artists working at No. 9 habitually ate at Chez Rosalie at no. 3, a modest restaurant founded on this location by

Chez Rosalie

Jockey Club

The Closerie des Lilas

The Closerie des Lilas, 1925

retired model Rosalie Tobia. (The building has since been demolished.)

26. On the west corner of rue Campagne Première and boulevard du Montparnasse was the original Jockey Club. Sarcastically co-opting the name of Paris's most exclusive sporting club for gentlemen, the Jockey was crudely decorated to resemble a western saloon. "Go at 11 o'clock", advised a contemporary guide book. "See famous painters and the real Bon Vivants of Paris. An indescribable atmosphere. A sign, reading 'The only client we ever lost, died'. Low, cracked ceilings and the tattered walls covered with posters. Cartoons painted with shoe polish."

Turn right on boulevard du Montparnasse and cross.

27. At 171, boulevard du Montparnasse (corner of boulevard du Montparnasse and boulevard St. Michel) is The Closerie des Lilas (The Garden of Lilacs), the last of the great Montparnasse cafés. Opened in 1847 as a stop on the main coach route out of Paris, it became a favorite of Montparnos. Émile Zola dined here with Paul Cézanne. Modigliani, Rimbaud, Apollinaire, Breton, Aragon, Picasso, Sartre, Gide, Eluard, Wilde, Beckett and Man Ray were all regulars. In 1922, the Dadaists put André Breton "on trial" here for attacking the founder of their movement, Tristan Tzara. Those who sided with Breton became the Surrealists. It was Hemingway's favorite workplace. He wrote "Big Two Hearted River" and "Soldier's Home" over café cremes in the calm of its hedge-enclosed terrace, and set parts of *The Sun Also Rises* there. Since then, the Closerie has gone up-market, dividing into an expensive restaurant and a more modest piano bar, the tables of which carry brass plates with the names (occasionally misspelled) of distinguished patrons from former times.

The Port Royal station opposite the Closerie des Lilas is served by the RER or overground railway. To return to central Paris, take one of the many buses that run down boulevard St. Michel.

THE STEINS COLLECT

One of the most famous art collections in the world began when Leo Stein rented a 460-square-foot studio and a two-bedroom apartment at 27, rue de Fleurus in Paris in 1903. Leo, together with his sister Gertrude, began buying paintings by Gauguin, Cézanne and Renoir in 1904. Within a few years they had collected hundreds of inexpensive paintings by a group of relatively unknown artists who also became their friends, including Matisse and Picasso. The Steins, together with their brother Michael and his wife Sarah, opened their apartments on Saturday evenings to artists, collectors, writers, and American expatriates. Those evenings went down in history as Gertrude Stein's famous salon, which introduced avant-garde art to the world.

Gertrude Stein, Pablo Picasso, 1905–06, The Metropolitan Museum of Art

Bathers, Paul Cézanne, 1898-1900, The Baltimore Museum of Art

Woman with a Hat, Henri Matisse, 1905, San Francisco Museum of Modern Art

Boy Leading a Horse, Pablo Picasso, 1905–06 , The Museum of Modern Art, New York

Boy with Butterfly Net, Henri Matisse, 1907, The Minneapolis Institute of Arts

IV. TROCADERO WALK

The area around Trocadero and the Palais de Chaillot has long associations with fashion, art and design, in particular Art Déco. The term "Art Déco" didn't come into general use until 1968, when it was coined by British art historian Bevis Hillier. As "déco" in French simply describes interior decoration of any sort, writers more conventionally referred to the new geometrical-based style typified by the 1925 Exposition internationale des Arts décoratifs et industriels modernes (The International Exhibition of Decorative and Industrial Arts) as "Arte Moderne."

① Eiffel Tower

② The Palais de Chaillot

③ The Varsovie Fountain

④ The former Cinématheque Française

⑤ Parvis des Droits de l'homme et des Libertés

⑥ The statue of George Washington
Place d'Iéna

⑦ Marché du pont de l'Alma

⑧ The Musée Galliera
10, avenue Pierre 1er de Serbie

⑨ Palais de Tokyo
11-13, avenue du President Wilson

⑩ Musée d'Art Moderne de la Ville de Paris
11, avenue du President Wilson

⑪ Site de Création Contemporaine
13, avenue du President Wilson

⑫ Fondation Pierre Bergé-Yves Saint Laurent
5, avenue Marceau
3, rue Léonce Reynaud

⑬ The Flame of Liberty

Ⓐ Théâtre des Champs-Élysées
15, avenue Montaigne

Ⓑ Guerlain's flagship boutique
68, avenue des Champs-Élysées

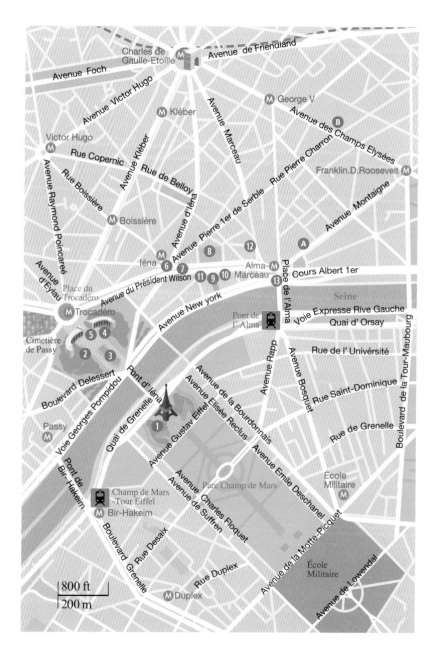

Charles de Gaulle-Etoile Ⓜ
Avenue de Friendland
Avenue Foch
Avenue Victor Hugo
Ⓜ George V
Avenue des Champs Elysées
Ⓜ Kléber
Avenue Marceau
Ⓑ
Victor Hugo Ⓜ
Rue Copernic
Rue de Belloy
Avenue Kléber
Rue Pierre Charron
Franklin.D.Roosevelt Ⓜ
Rue Boissière
Avenue Raymond Poincareé
Rue d'Iéna
Avenue Pierre 1er de Serble
Avenue Montaigne
Ⓜ Boissière
Ⓐ
⑧
⑫
Iéna Ⓜ ⑥ ⑦
Alma- Ⓜ
Place de l'Alma
Cours Albert 1er
Avenue d'Eylau
Avenue du Président Wilson ⑪ ⑨ ⑩
Marceau
⑬
Place du Trocadéro
Seine
Ⓜ Trocadéro
Avenue New york
Pont de l'Alma 🚆
Voie Express Rive Gauche
Quai d' Orsay
Cimetière de Passy
⑤ ④
Rue de l' Univérsité
② ③
Boulevard Delessert
Avenue Rapp
Avenue Bosquet
Rue Saint-Dominique
Boulevard de la Tour-Maubourg
Pont d'Iéna
Voie Georges Pompidou
Avenue de la Bourdonnais
Quai de Grenelle
Avenue Gustav Eiffel
Avenue Elisée Reclus
Rue de Grenelle
Passy Ⓜ
①
Avenue Emile Deschanel
École Militaire Ⓜ
Pont de Bir-Hakeim
Champ de Mars -Tour Eiffel 🚆
Avenue Charles Floquet
Parc Champ de Mars
Ⓜ Bir-Hakeim
Avenue de Suffren
Boulevard Grenelle
Rue Desaix
École Militaire
Rue Duplex
Avenue de la Motte-Picquet
Avenue de Lowendal
800 ft
200 m
Ⓜ Duplex

257

Start:
PER at Champ de Mars/
Tour Eiffel

End:
Métro at Alma Marceau

The Eiffel Tower

Gustave Eiffel

Citroën lighting

Paris Through the Window
(detail), Marc Chagall, 1913

Commence walk at the Eiffel Tower. The Tower is poorly served by public transport. The nearest station is the RER's Champ de Mars/Tour Eiffel. Otherwise, take the bus (69 or 87) or the Metro to École Militaire (Line 8), then walk to the Tower through the Champ de Mars.

1. The Eiffel Tower is situated on the Champ de Mars, a former parade ground for the nearby École Militaire military school. The tower was erected in 1889 as a temporary entrance to that year's International Exposition. Despite calls to demolish it, Gustave Eiffel's masterpiece has become an internationally recognized symbol for Paris, visited by 200 million people to date.

The tower has 704 steps. Most visitors prefer the elevators, though few go beyond the second-story observation deck. The summit houses Eiffel's restored office, with wax figures reproducing the occasion when Thomas Edison presented Eiffel with a phonograph. For the duration of World War I, the tower was fenced off for use as an aircraft beacon and radio transmission mast, a function that continues today. A searchlight on the summit still sweeps the sky at night, and TV and telephone antennae cluster on the summit.

During the 1925 Exposition, lights on the tower spelled out an advertisement for auto manufacturer Citroën. For the millennium celebrations in 2000, a web of twinkling halogen lamps covered the exterior. Like the tower, they proved too popular to remove, and now ignite for five minutes at the top of each hour.

Numerous 20th-century painters, authors and film-makers have used the tower, notably Jean Cocteau and the composers of Les Six for the 1921 ballet *The Wedding Party on the Eiffel Tower*, a subject also tackled by Marc Chagall in a 1913 canvas. René Clair's 1925 film *Paris qui dort* (*Paris Asleep*) shows an inventor's experiment freezing Paris into immobility. As the tower is out of range of the immobilizing ray, those unaffected retreat there to loaf and flirt.

The tower is open every day year-round, usually between 9:30am and 11pm. Tickets are required. Expect long waits both for tickets and elevators, particularly in warm weather. Restaurants on the tower include the Jules Verne, named for the author of *20,000 Leagues Under the Sea*. Author Guy de Maupassant liked to eat there, since "it is the only place in Paris where I don't have to look at the Eiffel Tower."

Eiffel Tower, 1929

Cross the Pont d'Iéna to Right Bank.

2. The Palais de Chaillot on the hilltop of Trocadero was built for the 1937 *Exposition Internationale des Arts et Techniques dans la vie Moderne*, replacing an earlier undistinguished building in "Moorish" style dating from 1878.

Pont d'Iéna

A classic of late Art Déco, designed by Léon Azéma, Jacques Carlu and Louis-Hippolyte Boileau, the 1937 complex originally housed the Cinématheque Française, France's national film museum and cinema, the anthropological Musée de l'Homme, and the Theatre National Populaire. Today, it's occupied by the Musée de la Marine, devoted to France's maritime history, and the Cité de l'Architecture, celebrating national monuments. The Cinematheque moved to Bercy, and while some exhibits of the Musée de l'Homme remain in place, many now reside in the Musée du Quai Branly. The basement, accessed from the Trocadero gardens, contains an aquarium, cinemas and restaurants.

The Palais de Chaillot

Cross avenue de New York to Place de Varsovie.

3. The Varsovie (Warsaw) Fountain is a decorative pool flanked by sculptures and fountains, and is an impressive example of high Art Déco. The sculptures include two matching stone groups on pedestals towards the southeastern end, *The Joy of Living*, by Léon-Ernest Drivier and *Youth* by Pierre Poisson. At the first level below the Palais de Chaillot are matching

The old Trocadéro palace

The Varsovie fountain

Bull and Deer

Former Cinématheque Française

L'affaire Langlois, 1968

La Nuit Américaine

View from Parvis des Droits de
l'homme et des Libertés

stone figures of *Man* by Pierre Traverse and *Woman* by Daniel Bacqué, both leaning against stone pedestals. Two gilded bronze fountain sculptures, *Bull and Deer* by Paul Jouve and *Horses and Dog* by Georges Guyot, stand in their own square basins. A 21-foot bronze *Apollo with lyre* is by Henri Bouchard and a matching bronze *Hercules with bull* by Albert Pommier. The fountains, which can project jets of water 50 meters in the air, are illuminated at night.

4. To the right and underneath the eastern wing of the Palais is the entrance to the former Cinématheque Française. It was through this door (which resembles the access to an underground garage) that such young critics as François Truffaut and Jean-Luc Godard entered to see the films, programmed by Cinématheque director Henri Langlois, which inspired the New Wave and, indirectly, the student revolution of 1968 when Culture Minister André Malraux dismissed Langlois. During a protest in front of the Cinematheque entrance, the militia stormed a crowd being addressed by actor Jean-Pierre Leaud. The event is recreated in Bernardo Bertolucci's film *The Dreamers,* which also shows Eva Green chained to the entrance doors. The same doors appear over the opening credits of Truffaut's film about the filmmaking process, *La Nuit Americaine* (*Day for Night*).

Ascend to central esplanade.

5. Parvis des Droits de l'homme et des Libertés (The Square of the Rights and Liberties of Man). Ostentatiously renamed after World War II, the paved area between the wings of the Palais offers a striking view of the Eiffel Tower and the Trocadero gardens. Adolf Hitler chose this point to survey a conquered Paris in 1940. Statues of an elephant and a rhinoceros that originally stood here were removed in 1937 and now decorate the forecourt of the Musée d'Orsay.

Exit onto Place Trocadero et du 11me Novembre. (The armistice that ended war with Germany was signed on November 11, 1918.) Turn right onto avenue du President Wilson and descend to Place d'Iéna.

6. The statue of George Washington, mounted, with sword raised, on Place d'Iéna is by Daniel Chester French. Paid for by the Daughters of the American Revolution, it was erected in 1900.

7. The Marché du pont de l'Alma is an open-air food and produce market, said to be the largest in Paris. The market takes place every Wednesday and Saturday morning, occupying much of the central island of avenue du President Wilson. It opens from about 7am to 2:30pm.

Walk around Place d'Iéna and enter avenue Pierre 1er de Serbie.

8. The Musée Galliera, which fills the Square Brignole Galliera between avenue du President Wilson and avenue Pierre 1er de Serbie contains the City of Paris Museum of Fashion. Opened in 1977, it occupies a Renaissance-style palace built at the end of the 19th century for the Duchesse de Galliera. The museum stages two exhibitions each year.

Return to avenue du President Wilson and cross to southern side.

9. Dating from 1937, the Palais de Tokyo, situated at 11-13 avenue du President Wilson, took its name from the former riverside avenue de Tokyo, now avenue de New York. It was built to house the national collection of modern art. Le Corbusier and Robert Mallet-Stevens both submitted designs, but a committee of architects finally opted for a plain concrete structure that would not distract attention from the art.

Statue of a rhinoceros

Statue of George Washington

Marché du pont de l'Alma

The Musée Galliera

Palais de Tokyo, 1937

Musée d'Art Moderne

Raoul Dufy's *The Electricity Fairy*

Site de Création Contemporaine

5, avenue Marceau

Yves Saint Laurent, 1974

10. The eastern wing at 11, avenue du President Wilson belongs to the city of Paris and contains the Musée d'Art Moderne de la Ville de Paris. As well as works by Matisse, Bonnard, Picabia, Vuillard, Delaunay and other artists associated with Paris, the museum contains Raoul Dufy's *The Electricity Fairy*. Commissioned for the 1937 Exposition, this panorama of 250 panels illustrates the history of electricity and its applications.

11. The western wing at 13, avenue du President Wilson belongs to the French state. Following the transfer of the national collection of modern art to the Centre Pompidou in 1977, this portion of the Palais became home to the film school FEMIS and other institutions, but fell into disrepair and was partially closed. Redesigned by Anne Lacaton and Jean-Philippe Vassal, it reopened in 2011 as a Site de Création Contemporaine, presenting a wide-ranging agenda of contemporary exhibitions, events and performance.

Descend avenue du President Wilson and turn left into avenue Marceau.

12. Created in memory of couturier Yves St. Laurent in his former home and office, the Fondation Pierre Bergé–Yves Saint Laurent occupies 5, avenue Marceau with an exhibition space and bookshop at 3, rue Léonce Reynaud. The museum preserves St. Laurent's apartment and studio, with a representative selection of his work, and offers guided tours by appointment. It also periodically presents exhibitions of paintings and photography.

Cross avenue de New York to pont de l'Alma.

13. *The Flame of Liberty* is a 3.5 metre sculpture in gilded copper, and is a facsimile of the flame held by the Statue of Liberty in New York. It was erected by the *New York Herald Tribune* in 1987 to commemorate 100 years of publication in Paris.

While driving through the underpass to the left of this intersection and beneath this monument, Diana, Princess of Wales, lost her life in an automobile accident on August 31, 1997. *The Flame of Liberty* sculpture has since become an ad hoc memorial to her memory. (*Note*: On no account attempt to enter the underpass itself, which is highly dangerous.)

Rejoin Metro at Alma Marceau station (Line 9).

The Flame of Liberty

Princess Diana memorial

INDEX

20,000 Leagues Under the Sea
    259
1924 Olympic 114
1924 Olympic Games 110, 112

A

Abrahams, Harold 113
absinthe 130, 133, 134, 137
Adenauer, Konrad 101
Adventure of the Creeping Man,
    The 96
A Farewell to Arms 243
After Leaving Mr. Mackenzie
    234
Agence Iris 89, 91
Aldington, Richard 233
Alexandre III bridge, the 143
Algeria 132
Algiers 99
Alice B. Toklas Cook Book, The
    137
Allain, Marcel 38, 40
Alma Marceau 263
Alsace 46
Ambroise Paré nursing home 99
A Moveable Feast 75, 244, 249
An American in Paris 164, 165,
    169
Anderson, Sherwood 73, 74,
    242, 250
Angkor Wat 108
Ansermet, Ernest 35
Antheil, George 55
Antibes 222, 224
apache 18, 21, 24
Apollinaire, Guillaume 41, 71,
    102
Aragon, Louis 11, 176, 192, 249
Arden, Elizabeth 67
Armory Show 76
Arp, Hans 190
Art Blakey's Jazz Messengers
    236
Art Déco 138, 141, 144, 145, 232
artificial paradises 130
Art Nouveau 141, 232
Atatürk, Mustafa Kemal 99
Atget, Eugene 129, 212, 246,
    253
Atherton, Gertrude 96, 101
Auberge de Venise 16, 246, 250

Auric, George 33
avenue des Champs-Elysées
    67, 256
avenue du President Wilson
    256, 261
avenue Foch 217
avenue Laplace 161
avenue Marceau 256, 262
Avenue Montaigne 99
avenue Pierre 1er de Serbie
    256, 261

B

Bacon, Francis 250
Baker, Joséphine 101, 109, 119,
    123, 127, 173, 176, 251
Bakst, Léon 31, 221
Balanchine, Georges 33
Baldwin, James 248
Ballets Russes 26, 29, 32, 34, 35,
    123, 181, 221
Balzac, Honoré de 235, 246, 248
Barbette 182, 183, 185
Barnes, Djuna 73, 180
Barney, Natalie Clifford 180
Bastille 20
Bathers 255
Baudelaire, Charles 132
Beach, Sylvia 52, 53, 54, 55, 56,
    58, 59, 73, 181, 202,
    206, 237, 238, 244, 245
Beat Generation 237
Beauvoir, Simone de 234, 246,
    250, 252
Beaux, Ernest 63
Bécat, Paul-Emile 82
Bechet, Sidney 123
Becker, Jacques 24
Beckett, Samuel 55, 233, 236,
    249, 252
Bedaux, Charles 108
Before Sunset 237
Beggars of Life 85
Beijing 106
Beirut 106
belle époque 132
Belleville 21, 22, 168
Bell, J.X. 167
Belmondo, Jean-Paul 150
Benois, Alexander 31
Bérard, Christian 73

Bergner, Elizabeth 157
Berlin 99, 178, 181
Berman, Eugene 73
Bibliothèque Forney 137
Biederbecke, Bix 125
Big Parade, The 213
Black Laughter 74
Black Oxen 96
Black Sun Press, The 207, 209
bob 78, 80, 81, 84
Bodenheim, Maxwell 84
bœuf 123, 127
Bogart, Humphrey 214
Bois de Boulogne 205, 217
Bois de Vincennes 108
Bonnard, Pierre 31, 32, 262
Bonnot Gang, the 39
Bordeaux 108
Boris Godunov 29
Borodin 32
Boston 204
Boswell, James 214
Boudu sauvé des eaux 232
Boulanger, Nadia 165
boulevard du Montparnase 238,
    241, 246, 248
boulevard Edgar Quinet 185,
    246
boulevard Raspail 246, 248
boulevard St. Germain 172,
    238, 244
boulevard St. Michel 235
Bourdelle, Antoine 142
Bourdet, Edouard 184
Bow, Clara 79, 80
Bowles, Paul 73, 74
Boy Leading a Horse 255
Boy with Butterfly Net 76, 255
Brandt, Edgar 142, 144
Branger, Maurice 171
Braque, Georges 33, 71, 102, 220
Brassai 125, 131, 135, 176, 179,
    183, 211, 214, 234, 251
Brasserie Lipp 172, 177, 238, 244
Braun, Eva 215
Brel, Jacques 235
Breton, André 11, 176, 190, 192,
    193, 234, 237, 250
Brooks, Louise 85, 128
Brooks, Romaine 181
Brousse, Roger 113

Bruce, Patrick Henry 71
Bruller, Jean 232
Bullard, Eugene 121, 127
Buñuel, Luis 81, 176, 186, 188, 189, 191, 192, 193, 248, 249, 252
Burroughs, Edgar Rice 101
Burroughs, William S. 136

C

Cabaret L'Écluse 230, 235
Café de Flore 177, 238, 243
Café de la Paix 215
Café Delmas 238, 240
Café Les Deux Magots 177, 238, 243
Café Pre aux Clercs 238, 244
Callaghan, Morley 57, 175, 196, 197, 198, 199, 200, 243
Campagne-Première, rue 11
Camus, Albert 157
Canary Islands 193
Cape of Good Hope 105
Captive, The 184
Carax, Leos 233
Carco, Francis 214
Carnegie Hall 165
Caron, Leslie 164, 169
Carrel, Alexis 97
Casque d'Or 22, 24, 25
Castanayer, Juan 248
Castle, Irene 79, 80, 118
Caveau de la Huchette 230, 236
Caveau des Innocents 24
Celine, Louis-Ferdinand 157
Cendrars, Blaise 41, 214
Censier Daubenton 240
Cézanne, Paul 71, 73, 74, 243, 254, 255
Chabrol, Claude 232
Chad 106
Chagall, Marc 258
Chamonix 115, 152
Champ de Mars 258
Champsaur, Félicien 101
Chanel, Coco 34, 35, 63, 66, 150, 223, 226
Chanel No. 5 64
Chaplin, Charlie 101
Chardin, Teilhard de 106
Chariots of Fire 110

Charleston 118, 119, 122
Charters, Jimmie 75
Chautemps, Camille 152
Chevalier, Maurice 18, 21, 166, 176
Chez Bricktop 122, 123, 127
Chez Joséphine 127
Chez Rosalie 246, 253
Chez Suzy 211
Chiappe, Jean 152
Chirico, Giorgio de 176, 253
Christo 233
Cimetière du Montparnasse 16, 246, 252
Cinematheque Française 193, 256, 259, 260
Cité de l'Architecture 259
Cité des Artistes 246, 253
Citroën, André 104, 105, 106, 107, 108, 109, 142, 258
Clair, René 258
Claridge's Hotel 150
Closerie des Lilas 16, 175, 177, 238, 241, 246, 254
Clouzot, Henri-Georges 235
Clyde, Vander. See Barbette
Cocéa, Alice 107
Cocteau, Jean 12, 33, 34, 120, 123, 126, 127, 135, 181, 183, 223, 224, 226, 258
Colette 180
Colin, Paul 122
Comedie Française, the 170
Comptoir des Saints-Pères, Le (Michaud's) 238, 244
Cone, Claribel 71
Cone, Etta 71
Cone sisters 73
Congo 106, 124
Contact Press 185, 197, 206, 238, 245
Corso, Gregory 237
Côte d'Azur 26, 34, 222, 226
Coty, François 65, 144
Coward, Noel 101
Crane, Hart 13, 248
Crevel, René 190
Croisière Blanche, La 107, 108
Croisière Jaune, La 106, 107

Croisière Noire, La 103, 105
Crosby, Caresse 135, 136, 202, 203, 205, 207, 238
Crosby, Harry 202, 203, 205, 207, 208, 238
Cubist 33, 71, 74, 140, 141, 220
Cummings, E.E. 54
Cunard, Nancy 233

D

Dada Excursion 237
Dakar-Djibouti Expedition 107, 109
Daladier, Edouard 152
Dalí, Salvador 16, 81, 176, 186, 188, 189, 190, 191, 192, 216, 249
Danton 172
Darantiere, Maurice 56
Daven, André 122
de Coubertin, Baron Pierre 110, 115
de Gaulle, Charles 105, 232
de la Serna, Ismael 248
Delaunay, Robert 262
de Molay, Jacques 233
Deneuve, Catherine 236, 252
Derain, André 33, 176
Desire Caught by the Tail 230, 234
Desnos, Robert 41
Diaghilev, Serge 26, 28, 29, 31, 32, 33, 34, 35, 99, 164, 181, 221, 226
Diana, Princess of Wales 263
Diary of a Lost Girl 85
Dickens, Charles 4
Dietrich, Marlene 84, 214
Die Unbekannte 157
Dingo Bar 16, 75, 196, 250
Dodge, Mabel 72
Dôme, the 13, 16, 175, 177, 246, 249
Doolittle, Hilda 185
Dos Passos, John 54
Doyle, Conan 96
Drosso's 135, 136, 205
Ducasse, Isidore 251
Duchamp, Marcel 10, 253
Dufy, Raoul 262
Duke of Westminster 223

Duke, Vernon 164
Dunand, Jean 142
Duncan, Isadora 246, 250
Dupas, Jean 142
Duret, Francisque-Joseph 235
Durrell, Lawrence 214, 237

E

Edison, Harry "Sweets" 236
Edmonton 107
Egypt 97, 104, 157
Ehrman, Theresa 70
Eiffel, Gustav 148, 258
Eiffel Tower 109, 128, 142, 145,
        146, 149, 256, 258, 260
Elbe, Lily 99
Electricity Fairy, The 262
Ellerman, Annie Winifred 185
Ellington, Duke 125, 213, 251
Éluard, Paul 11, 42, 190, 193
Ernst, Max 11, 190, 209
Europe, James Reese 118, 120
Exposition Coloniale
        Internationale 108
Exposition des Arts Décoratifs
        Paris 140, 143
Exposition Internationale des
        Arts et Techniques
        dans la vie Moderne
        259
Exposition Universelle 148

F

Fantômas 36, 38, 40, 42
Ferlinghetti, Lawrence 237
Feuillade, Louis 40, 42, 43
Firebird 32
Fitzgerald, Scott 57, 73, 80, 196,
        197, 198, 199, 200,
        218, 221, 223, 226,
        238, 242, 244, 250
Fitzgerald, Zelda 218, 219, 223,
        238, 242, 244
Flame of Liberty, The 256, 262
Flaming Youth 79, 80
Flanner, Janet 13, 180
Folies Bergère 48, 49, 119, 123
Fondation Pierre Bergé-Yves
        Saint Laurent 256, 262
Fontainebleau 165
Foujita, Tsuguharu 9, 16, 214,

246, 249, 250
Four Figurines on a Base 214
Franklin, Benjamin 170
Fratellini clown brothers 123
French, Breton 109
French Music School for
        Americans 165

G

Gainsbourg, Serge 252
Gallardo, Manolo 113
Galleries Lafayette 142
Gambais 91, 92, 93
Garbo, Greta 4, 157
Garches 76
Gare de Lyon 226
Gare Saint-Lazare 10
Gauguin, Paul 250, 255
Gershwin, George 163, 164,
        165, 169
Giacometti, Alberto 214, 249
Gibran, Khalil 248
Gide, André 57, 106, 181
Gilmore, Buddy 120
Gilot, Françoise 72
Ginsberg, Allen 4, 237
Girodias, Maurice 236
Gobi Desert 106
Godard, Jean-Luc 260
Goldman, Emma 248
Gontcharova, Natalia 220
Goodsir, Australian Agnes 181
Gotha bombers 48
Grand Guignol 49
Grand Hôtel 47
Grand Palais 140, 141
Grands Magasins du Louvre 65
Granet, André 144
Grant, Cary 166, 214
Grappelli, Stéphane 126
Great Gatsby, The 57, 197
Gris, Juan 71, 73, 220
Guerlain, Jacques 60, 65
Guerlain's flagship boutique
        256
Guernica 235
Guilbert, Yvette 181
Gysin, Bryon 136

H

Haardt, Georges-Marie 105,

106, 108
Hall, Adelaide 124
Hall, Radclyffe 180
Hamnett, Nina 10
Hampton, Lionel 236
Harburg, E.Y. 164
Harrods 132
Harry's New York Bar 165, 169
Haussmann, Baron Georges-
        Eugene 8, 145, 172
Hayter, Stanley 253
Heap, Jane 12
Hemingway, Ernest 54, 55, 57,
        58, 68, 72, 73, 74, 75,
        185, 194, 195, 196,
        197, 198, 199, 200,
        201, 204, 205, 238,
        240, 241, 242, 244,
        245, 249, 250, 254
Hemingway, Hadley 74, 75, 240,
        241, 244
Himalayas 106, 108
Hitler, Adolf 215, 260
Hoffman Girls, The 128
Hong Kong 106
Hot Club of France, the 126
Hôtel Aiglon 193, 246, 252
Hôtel d'Angleterre 238, 244
Hôtel Delambre 246, 250
Hôtel des Bains 250
Hôtel des Invalides 140
Hôtel des Monnaies 230
Hôtel des Terrasses 193
Hôtel d'un Collectionneur, the
        139, 142
Hôtel Istria 246, 253
Hôtel Lenox 246, 250
Hours Press 230, 233
Huddleston, Sisley 12
Hudson, Hugh 110
Hughes, Langston 121
Hugo, Victor 235
Human Voice, The 181

I

Idylle Saphique 180
Île de la Cité 154, 158
Île Saint-Louis 230
Innocents of Paris 166
Ionesco, Eugene 236
Irma Vep 42, 43

Isherwood, Christopher 178, 181
Island of Doctor Moreau, The 101
Issy-les-Moulineaux 117
It 80

J

Jaureguy, Adolphe 113
Jazz Plantation Orchestra, the 124
Jeanneret, Pierre 145
Jicky 62, 66
Jockey Club 246, 254
Jourdain, Frantz 232
Joyce, James 16, 52, 53, 55, 59, 73, 236, 244
Judex 42, 43
Jules et Jim 11
Jules Verne 259

K

Kangourou, Makoko 123
Karsavina, Tamara 27
Kashmir 106
Kégresse, Adolphe 104
Kelly, Gene 164, 169
Kiki 9, 12, 16, 253
King Ibn Saoud 101
Kisling, Moise 176, 214, 249, 253
Kochno, Boris 35, 168
Kohner, Frederick 60

L

La Baionnette 49
La Boule Blanche 125
La Coupole 13, 16, 175, 177, 246, 248
La Fée Verte 137
L'Afrique fantôme 108
La Garçonne 80, 82, 83, 84, 184
La Grande Severine 230, 236
La Java 129
Lalique, René 142, 144
La Maison des Amis des Livres 54
Landé, Jean-Baptiste 26
Landru, Henri-Desire 88, 89, 90, 92
Lang, Eddie 125
Langlois, Henri 260

La Nuit Americaine (Day for Night) 260
La Perouse 230, 235
La Petite Chaumiere 183
La Prisonnière 184
La Revue Negre 122
La Rose Jacqueminot 65
La Samaritaine 230, 232
Last Nights of Paris, The 232
Last Time I Saw Paris, The 236
Latin Quarter, The 81, 235, 236
Laurencin, Marie 71
La Vie Parisienne 46
Lawrence, D. H. 207
Leca 22, 25
Le Chabanais 216, 217
Le Corbusier 76, 145, 261
LeGallienne, Richard 156
Léger, Fernand 122, 129, 176, 221, 249
Le Grand Duc 121, 127
Le Havre 117
Leiris, Michel 107, 109
le jazz frais 126
le jazz hot 118, 124, 126, 127
Le Livre Blanc 181
Le Mistral 59, 237
Le Monocle 128, 179, 183, 185, 215, 246, 251
Lenin, Vladimir Ilyich 248, 249
Le Panier Fleuri 230, 236
Le Petit Journal 20
Lerbier, Monique 80
Les Amants de Pont Neuf 233
Les Années Folles 4, 18, 149, 176, 185
Les Demoiselles d'Avignon 71
Les Halles 24
les Montparnos 176
Les Noces 221
Les Six 123, 126, 258
Les Vampires 40, 41, 43
Le Train Bleu 34
L'Etranger 157
Lewis, Sinclair 250
Lew Leslie's Black Birds 124
L'Heure Bleue 60
Liane de Pougy 180
Liddell, Eric 111, 113, 271
Lifar, Serge 35
L'Inconnue de la Seine 156, 157,

159, 160, 161, 232
Lindsay, Vachel 123
Little Review, The 55
Lolita 83, 159, 236
London 170
Lorca, Federico Garcia 189, 191
Lorenzi's 160, 161
L'Origan 66
Louvre 146, 230
Love Me Tonight 165
Loy, Mina 12
Lustig, Victor 146, 148, 153
Luxembourg gardens 54, 90, 238, 241

M

MacLeish, Archibald 205, 225, 243
Madagascar 105
Magic City 183, 184, 185
Magritte, Rene 41
Mailer, Norman 197, 200
maison closes 210, 212, 213, 215, 217
Maldoror, Le 246, 251
Mallet-Stevens, Robert 145, 261
Mallin, Harry 113
Malraux, André 105, 260
Man Ray 10, 12, 16, 69, 81, 102, 176, 182, 183, 190, 192, 214, 216, 223, 246, 249, 250, 252, 253
Marais, Jean 181
Marat, Jean-Paul 172
Marceau, Marcel 235
Marché du pont de l'Alma 256, 261
Margueritte, Victor 80, 81, 82, 83, 84, 184
Marquise de Lafayette 50
marraines de guerre 49, 89
Marrast, Joseph 142
Massine, Leonid 32, 33, 120
Masson, André 11
Matisse, Henri 33, 70, 71, 73, 76, 77, 249, 255, 262, 271
Maupassant, Guy de 235, 259
Maurer, Alfred 71
Maxim's 128
McAlmon, Robert 56, 57, 185,

195, 197, 206, 238, 245, 249
Memphis Slim 236
Menilmontant 168
Messan, Fano 81, 82, 191
Michaud 55
Midnight in Paris 5, 237
Milhaud, Darius 123
Miller, Henry 13, 146, 214, 248, 249, 250, 251
Miller, Lee 253
Miró, Joan 11
Miss Otis Regrets 122
Mistinguett 150, 176, 214
Mitsouko 63
Modigliani, Amadeo 10, 11, 141, 249, 253
Modvet, Maurice 24
Monaco 127
Mona Lisa 146, 157
Monnier, Adrienne 54, 55, 57, 59, 73, 181, 238, 245
Montand, Yves 230, 234
Monte Carlo 33
Montmartre 21, 121, 124
Montmartre Cemetery 35
Moore, Colleen 79, 80
Morocco 132, 136
Moser horticultural company 142
Moulin Rouge 124, 128
Mount Everest 115
Moysès, Louis 123
Murphy, Gerald 167, 218, 220, 221, 225, 226, 227, 238, 242
Murphy, Sara 218, 220, 221, 224, 238, 242
Muschler, Reinhold Conrad 157
Musée Carnavalet, the 137
Musée d'Art Moderne de la Ville de Paris 256, 262
Musée de la Marine 259
Musée de l'Erotisme 217
Musée de l'Homme 109, 259
Musée des Arts Decoratifs 31, 137
Musée d'Ethnographie 109
Musée d'Orsay 160, 260
Musée du Fumeur 137
Musée du Luxembourg 74,

238, 242
Musée du Montparnasse 16
Musée du Quai Branly 259
Musée Galliera 256, 261
Musée Nationale des Arts d'Afrique et d'Océanie 108
Museum of Death 93
Musidora 40, 43

N
Nabokov, Vladimir 83, 159, 236
Nadja 234
Nepalese 115
Neruda, Pablo 233
New Review, The 246
New York Herald Tribune 199, 215
Nice 26, 42, 100
Niehans, Dr. Paul 100
Night and Day 166
Nijinsky, Vaslav 27, 31, 32, 183
Nin, Anaïs 159
Ninotchka 4
Nogent-sur-Oise 99
Noiret, Philippe 235
Nora 99
Notre Dame 59, 154, 158, 161
Nurmi, Paavo 115, 116

O
Old Spice 67
Olivier, Fernande 71
Opera Garnier 35
opium 131, 135, 205
Orwell, George 240
Ouha, Roi des Singes 101

P
Pabst, G. W. 85
Palais de Chaillot 109, 145, 256, 259
Palais de Justice 233
Palais de la Cité 233
Palais de Tokyo 256, 261
Pandora's Box 85
Papeteries Gaubert 230, 234
Parade 33, 120, 221
Paris de Nuit 252
Paris qui dort (Paris Asleep) 258
Parker, Dorothy 223

Parvis des Droits de l'homme et des Libertés 256, 260
Pascin, Jules 214, 249
Passage d'Enfer, The 246, 253
Passos, John Dos 223, 250
Pastonchi, Francis 34
Paul, Elliott 236
Peabody, Polly 204
Perles, Alfred 13, 250
Pershing, John 50
Petain, Philippe 50
Petrushka 32, 35
Pfeiffer, Pauline 74, 196, 238, 243
Piaf, Edith 129, 168
Picabia, Francis 237, 253, 262
Picasso, Pablo 11, 33, 71, 72, 73, 76, 102, 220, 221, 223, 224, 226, 230, 234, 248, 249, 255
Pigalle 168
pinard 133
Place Blanche 173
Place Contrescarpe 238, 240
Place Dauphine 230, 233, 234
Place d'Iéna 256, 261
Place Jean Paul Sartre/Simone de Beauvoir 238, 243
Place Joséphine Baker 127, 246, 251
Place Saint Michel 230, 235
Place Saint Sulpice 243
Place Vendôme 65
Poe, Edgar Allan 207
Point, Victor 106
Poiret, Paul 11, 32, 143, 144
Pons, Lily 99
pont de l'Alma 262
Pont des Arts 230, 232
Pont de Sully 230
Pont Neuf 230, 232, 233
Pope Pius XII 101
Porgy and Bess 165
Porter, Cole 35, 121, 166, 167, 169, 222, 223, 242
Port Royal 254
Poulenc, Francis 33, 120, 123
Pound, Ezra 12, 16, 73, 146, 194, 196, 233, 249, 250
Prejean, Albert 168
Prin, Alice 102, 176, 249, 253. See also Kiki

Princess Grace 127
Procope 170, 238
Prokofiev, Sergei 33, 164
Proust, Marcel 47, 181, 207, 213
Putnam, Samuel 249

Q

Quai de Conti 233
Quai de l'Archevêché 161
Quai des Grands-Augustins 230, 234, 235
Quai des Orfevres 233, 235
Quai du Louvre 156, 158, 161, 232
Quiet Days in Clichy 250

R

Radiguet, Raymond 181, 249
Ravel, Maurice 165
Reagan, Caroline Dudley 123
Red Shoes, The 35
Red Skeletons 206
Reinhardt, Django 125, 126
Renoir, Jean 232
Renoir, Pierre-Auguste 255
Replenishing Jessica and Flaming Youth 84
Resnais, Alain 150
Resusci Anne 161
Rhys, Jean 234
Richard, Marthe 217, 251
Riding, Laura 233
Rilke, Rainer Maria 157
Rimbaud, Arthur 253
Rimsky-Korsakov 29, 31, 32
Rite of Spring 32
Ritz Hotel 65, 245
Robeson, Paul 101
Robespierre 172
Robinson, Bill "Bojangles" 120
Roché, Henri-Pierre 11
Rocky Mountains 107, 108
Rodin, Auguste 92, 248
Rosebud Bar 246, 250
Rotch, Josephine 207, 208
Rotonde, the 13, 16, 173, 174, 175, 177, 246, 248
Round Midnight 127
Rousseau, Jean-Jacques 102, 106, 108
Rudomine, Albert 155

rue Ancienne Comédie 238
rue Asselin 129
rue Auber 47
rue Boissy d'Anglas 127
rue Bonaparte 238, 244
rue Cambon 67
rue Campagne Première 246, 253
rue Cardinale 207, 209
rue Cardinal-Lemoine 238, 240
rue Danou 165, 169
rue de Fleurus 70, 71, 73, 74, 76, 137, 238, 242
rue de la Bucherie 230, 237
rue de la Gaite 127
rue de la Huchette 230, 235, 236
rue Delambre 11, 16, 246
rue de la Montagne-Sainte-Geneviève 93
rue de Lappe 25, 185
rue de la Roquette 137
rue de Lille 204, 209, 238
rue de l'Odéon 54, 55, 59, 237, 245
rue de Rennes 172
rue de Rivoli 137
rue Descartes 238, 241
rue de Sevigne 137
rue des Grands-Augustins 230, 234
rue des Saints-Pères 238, 244
rue de Vaugirard 238, 242
rue du Colisée 127
rue du Figuer 137
rue Férou 238, 243
rue Fontaine 121, 124, 127
rue Galande 230, 237
rue Guénégaud 230, 233
rue Guynemer 238, 242
rue Henri Robert 233
rue Jacob 180, 238, 244
rue Jean-Baptiste Pigalle 127
rue Léonce Reynaud 256, 262
rue Madame 76, 238
rue Mallet-Stevens 145
rue Monsieur 169
rue Mouffetard 238, 240
rue Nélaton 117
rue Notre Dame des Champs 249
rue Pache 137

rue Pigalle 121, 124, 127
rue Racine 160
rue Saint Séverin 230, 236
Ruhlmann, Emile-Jacques 139, 142, 144

S

Sahara 105
Saint Julien le Pauvre 230, 237
Salmon, André 11
Salon d'Automne 76, 81
Sand, George 235
Sartre, Jean-Paul 234, 250, 252
Satie, Erik 33, 120
Savoy Cocktail Book, The 138
Scheherezade 29, 221
Schirmer, Robert and Mabel 165
Seabrook, William 11, 216
Select, the 13, 16, 175, 177, 246, 248
Seurat, Georges 31
Shakespeare and Company 52, 53, 55, 57, 58, 59, 181, 202, 206, 230, 237, 245
Shanghai Express 84
Sheherazade 29, 31
Signoret, Simone 25, 230, 234
Silence of the Sea, The 232
Simenon, Georges 176, 214, 233
Sissle, Noble 120
Site de Création Contemporaine 256, 262
Smith, Ada "Bricktop" 121, 127
Snyder, Gary 237
Solonge, Madeleine 214
Sougez, Emmanuel 82
Soupault, Philippe 11, 230, 232, 237
Sous les Toits de Paris 168
Soutime, Chaim 249
Souvestre, Pierre 38, 40
Soviet Union 106
Sphinx, The 213, 214, 215, 217, 246, 251
Spock, Benjamin 115
Square du Docteur-Blanche 145
Stade Olympique in Colombes 117
Statue of Henri IV 230, 233
Stavisky, Serge 146, 150, 151, 153, 215

Steichen, Edward 77, 163, 271
Steinach, Eugen 94, 96, 100
Stein, Allan 70, 76, 77
Stein, Gertrude 68, 69, 70, 71,
72, 73, 74, 75, 76, 77,
130, 180, 185, 236,
238, 242, 255
Stein, Leo 70, 71, 76, 255
Stein, Michael 70, 76, 238, 255
Stein, Roubina 77
Stein, Sarah 70, 76, 238, 255
Stravinsky, Igor 32, 33, 35, 165,
221, 224, 226
Strutt, Lieutenant Colonel
Edward 115
Sun Also Rises, The 201, 242,
254
Surrealism 189, 237
Surrealist 10, 41, 107, 173, 190,
192, 193, 232

T
Tangiers 74
Tanguy, Yves 190
Tarzan 115
Tarzan of the Apes 101
Tavernier, Bertrand 127
Tchelitchew, Pavel 73
Tender Is the Night 218, 221,
223, 225, 226, 242
That Summer in Paris 198
Theatre de Champs-Elysées
123, 256
Theatre de la Huchette 230, 236
Theatre National Populaire 259
This Must Be the Place 75
Three Stories and Ten Poems

245
Tih-Minh 42
Toklas, Alice B. 68, 69, 71, 72, 73,
74, 75, 77, 136, 180,
238, 242
Tomboy, The 81
Torrents of Spring, The 74
Trocadero 109, 256, 259, 260
Truffaut, François 260
Tzara, Tristan 12, 190, 237, 250

U
Ulysses 52, 55, 56, 59, 244
Unamuno, Miguel de 248
Un Chien Andalou 81, 186,
192, 249
Unknown Virgin, The 155
Urumqi 106

V
Van Dongen, Kees 33
Vanity's Price 96
Varsovie Fountain, The 256, 259
Vassilieff, Marie 16
Vavin 248
Venice 34, 207
Venuti, Joe 125
Verlaine, Paul 241, 253
Versailles 86, 93, 212
Vichy 75
Vienna 94, 170
Villa America 222, 223, 225, 226
Villa Grimaldi 34, 98, 99, 100
Villa Molière 99
von Horváth, Ödön 159
Voronoff, Serge 34, 94, 95, 97,
98, 99, 100

Vuillard, Edouard 31, 262

W
Walk A Little Faster 164
Washington, George 256, 261
Wasp and Pear 218, 225, 227
Watt and Molloy 236
Wechsberg, Joseph 124
Wedding Party on the Eiffel
Tower, The 258
Wegener, Gerda 99
Weissmuller, Johnny 115
Well of Loneliness, The 180
Wells, H.G. 101
Wertheimers 66
Wharton, Edith 44, 51
Wheeler, Dr. Clayton E. 98
Whistler, James McNeil 4, 253
Whitman, George 59, 237
Wilde, Oscar 178, 180, 181
Wilder, Thornton 73, 250
Woman With a hat 76, 255
Wonder Bar 210
World's Most Beautiful Swindles,
The 153

Y
Yeats, W.B. 94

Z
Zadkine, Ossip 249
Zephyr and Flora 164
Zeppelin 46
Zola, Émile 235, 254

CREDITS

ABOUT MUSEYON

Named after the Museion, the ancient Egyptian institute dedicated to the muses, Museyon Guides is an independent publisher that explores the world through the lens of cultural obsessions. Intended for frequent fliers and armchair travelers alike, our books are expert-curated and carefully researched, offering rich visuals, practical tips and quality information.

MUSEYON'S OTHER TITLES

Publisher: Akira Chiba
Editor: Janice Battiste   Proof Editor: Mackenzie Allison

Cover Design: José Antonio Contreras
Marketing Manager: Maria Bukhonina

Museyon Guides has made every effort to verify that all information included in this guide is accurate and current as of our press date. All details are subject to change.

ABOUT THE AUTHOR

John Baxter is an Australian-born writer, journalist and filmmaker; he has called Paris home since 1989. He is the author of numerous books including the autobiographical *Immoveable Feast: A Paris Christmas*, *We'll Always Have Paris: Sex and Love in the City of Light*, *The Most Beautiful Walk in the World: A Pedestrian in Paris* and *Chronicles of Old Paris: Exploring The Historic City of Light*.